TIMELESS ART

Indian Art Series

TIMELESS ART

Poosapati Parameshwar Raju

MOSA
MUSEUM OF SACRED ART

NIYOGI BOOKS

MOSA

MUSEUM OF SACRED ART

Director
Martin Gurvich
Curator
Sushma K. Bahl
General Manager
Raymond Hoogenboom
Collections
Anushka Hoogenboom
Publishing
Phelelani Mdabe
Website
Dario Knez

Belgium
General Manager
Raymond Hoogenboom
Reception
Maria Grison • Patience Offei • Bergita Gjergjaj

Château de Petite Somme, B-6940, Septon (Durbuy), Belgium
t: +32 (0)86 43 30 22 • *e*: info@mosabelgium.com • www.mosabelgium.com

Italy
General Manager
Patrizio Landolfi

Via Scopeti 106/108, San Casciano in Val di Pesa, 50026, Florence, Italy
t: +39 (055) 82 00 54 • *e*: info@mosaitaly.com • www.mosaitaly.com

Catalog
Texts
Sushma K. Bahl
Designer
Phelelani Mdabe
Photography
Param P. Tomanec • Sushma K. Bahl

ISBN: 978-93-83098-45-3

Marketed world wide by

NIYOGI BOOKS

D-78, Okhla Industrial Area, Phase-I, New Delhi-110 020, INDIA
Tel: 91-11-26816301, 49327000, Fax: 91-11-26810483, 26813830
Email: niyogibooks@gmail.com, Website: www.niyogibooksindia.com

CONTENTS

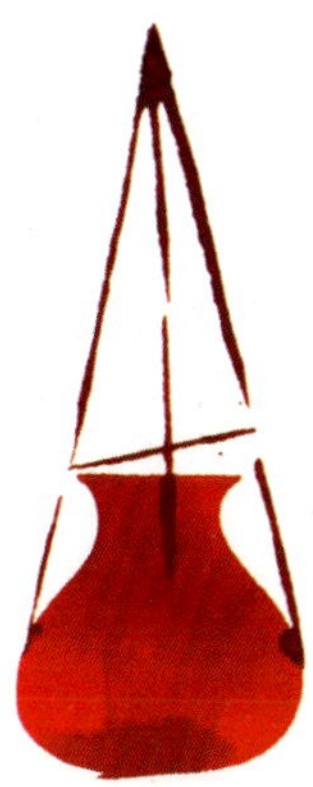

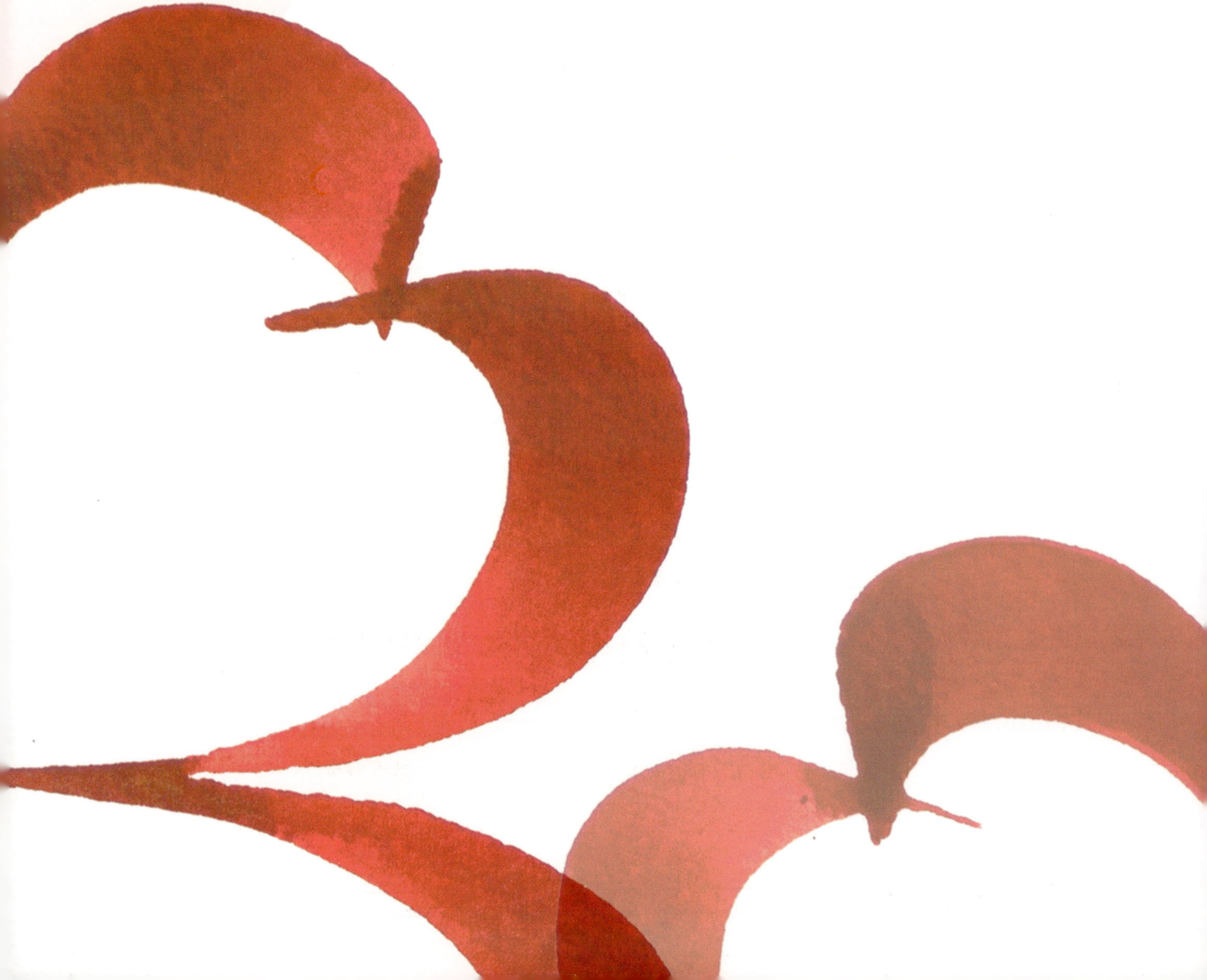

FOREWORD

Ambassador

भारतीय राजदूतावास
EMBASSY OF INDIA
CHAUSSEE DE VLEURGAT, 217
1050, BRUXELLES
TEL. 640 91 40
FAX 648 96 38

March 10, 2014

MESSAGE

"I am delighted that the prestigious Museum of Sacred Art is organizing exhibitions of three prominent Indian artists in Belgium aimed at amalgamating different forms of spirituality associated with diverse global faiths through fine arts.

The theme of the exhibitions—Forms of Devotion—is apt in the context of the expositions that celebrate the multiplicity, diversity, creativity and vibrancy of devotional art of India in varied hues and forms. The unique paintings and calligraphic works of the Indian artists--Posapati Parameshwar Raju, Raghupati Bhat and Shobha Broota—transcend faiths and genres—figurative, mythological, abstract, Hindu, Muslim, Christian, Sikh, Buddhist, Jain etc – and showcase the dynamic multi-religious and multi-cultural life of India to the west.

The antiquity of Indian civilization matched by the vastness of its geographical extent has contributed to the rich and multiple art forms of India. These art forms have been successfully presented by the Museum of Sacred Art not only in Belgium, but also in the whole of Europe over the last five years since its inception. I deeply appreciate the initiative of the Museum to encourage interfaith dialogue through fine arts as manifested in these upcoming exhibitions.

I am confident that the Indian art- loving people of Europe would once again have the opportunity to witness Indian mythology, icons and folk tales through the forthcoming exhibitions and that too after the just concluded Europalia-India Festival.

I convey my best wishes to the Museum of Sacred Art of Belgium for a successful organization of the forthcoming exhibitions".

(M.S. Puri)

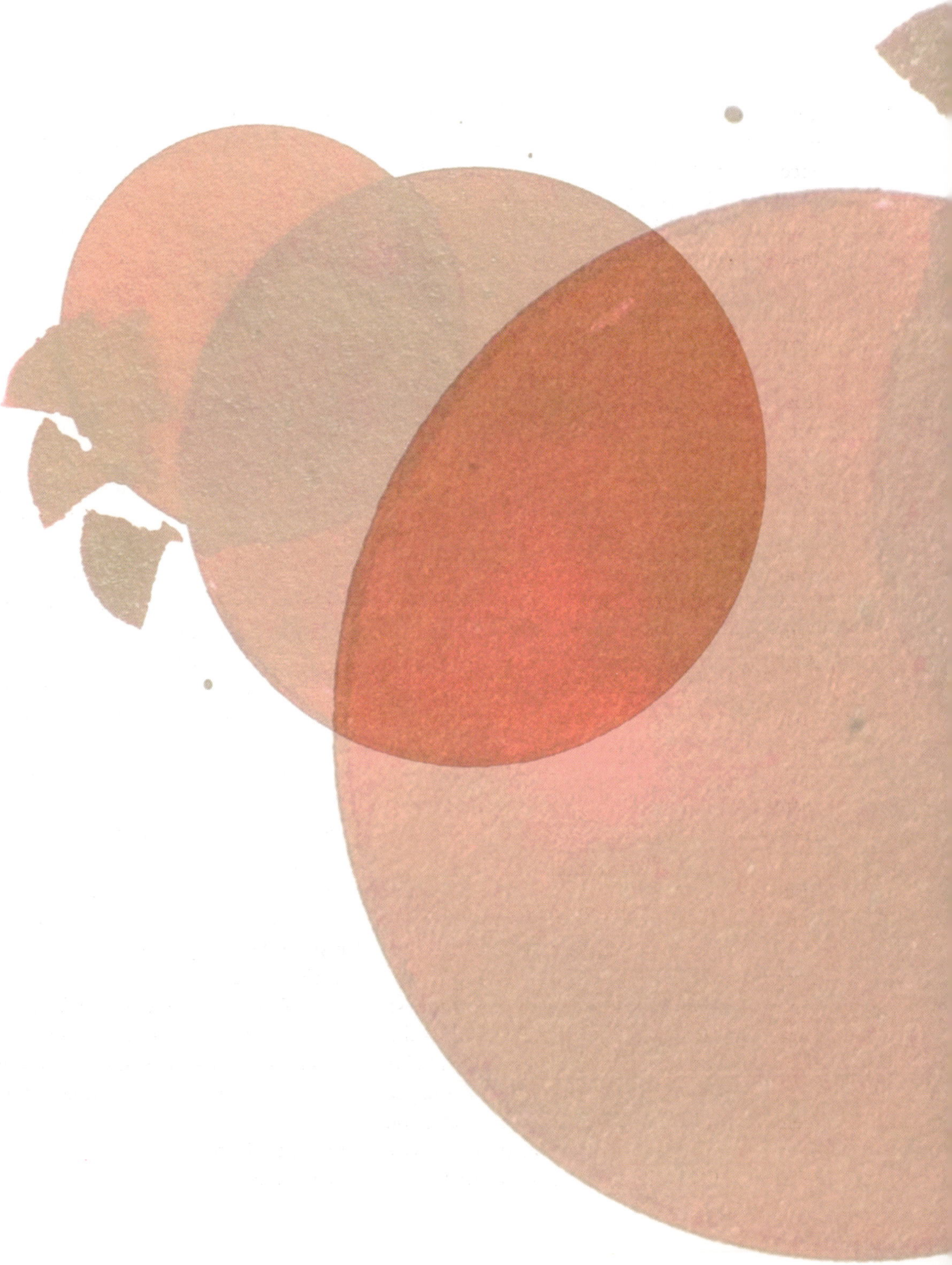

PREFACE

The prospect of inaugurating the 2014 art exhibits at MOSA with such outstanding, accomplished artists as Shobha Broota, Raghupati Bhat, and Poosapati Parameshwar Raju fills me with profound joy. The inauguration will be attended by our guest of honor His Excellency M.S. Puri, ambassador of India to Belgium and the EU, and art curator Sushma K. Bahl, who has written the texts about all three artists. Moreover, this festive event will be graced by musical performances by celebrated flautist Panditji Hariprasad Chaurasia and renowned sitar player Subrata De. Our exhibition program for Indian and International artists working on spiritual, devotional and sacred art is quite dynamic and our galleries in Belgium (Radhadesh, Durbuy) and Italy (Villa Vrindavan, Florence) will be showcasing many of them in the upcoming years.

MOSA's goal is to bridge the cultural divide between India and Europe and between material and spiritual life. Art is a perfect medium to do so, and we hope that many Europeans will discover the excellent Indian artists who try to convey a spiritual message. We are convinced that MOSA's visitors will come to appreciate and enjoy the currently exhibited work of all three artists.

Poosapati Parameshwar Raju brings us Lord Rama and Lord Krishna in a subtle yet captivating way. This is calligraphy at its best. Parameshwar Raju expertly fuses the world of words with the world of images, and captured in his strokes and delicate lines, the Ramayana seems to transcend both worlds. His series on World Faiths closely brings together symbols of various faiths, which reminds us that although there may be differences between different faiths, there are also similarities. Of course, considering all faiths to be the same is erroneous, but to pride oneself on being different and fight over religious matters is likewise mistaken and simply expressive of a neophyte and shallow understanding of the various faiths.

At MOSA we hope that the art we exhibit will contribute to a greater understanding and appreciation among the various faiths, so that they may all work together for the betterment of human society. By encouraging followers to understand and sincerely practice the teachings of their particular tradition, let us all eradicate whatever indifference towards spiritual progress still lingers within us, but let us not overemphasize or condemn the differences in our practices and theologies. Let us dialogue and cooperate to make the world a place free of greed, anger, lust, fear, envy, and so on.

Parameshwar Raju's art is a guide toward such dialogue and cooperation. And it is wonderfully complemented by Raghupati Bhat's work with which it shares gallery space. May this exhibition inspire MOSA visitors to discover an ancient culture, and may it inspire them to go deeper in introspection and spiritual reflection.

We are also delighted and honored that Parameshwar Raju will attend the opening of MOSA's 2014 art exhibits, and that he will demonstrate his skills to the other attendees.

Martin Gurvich
Director

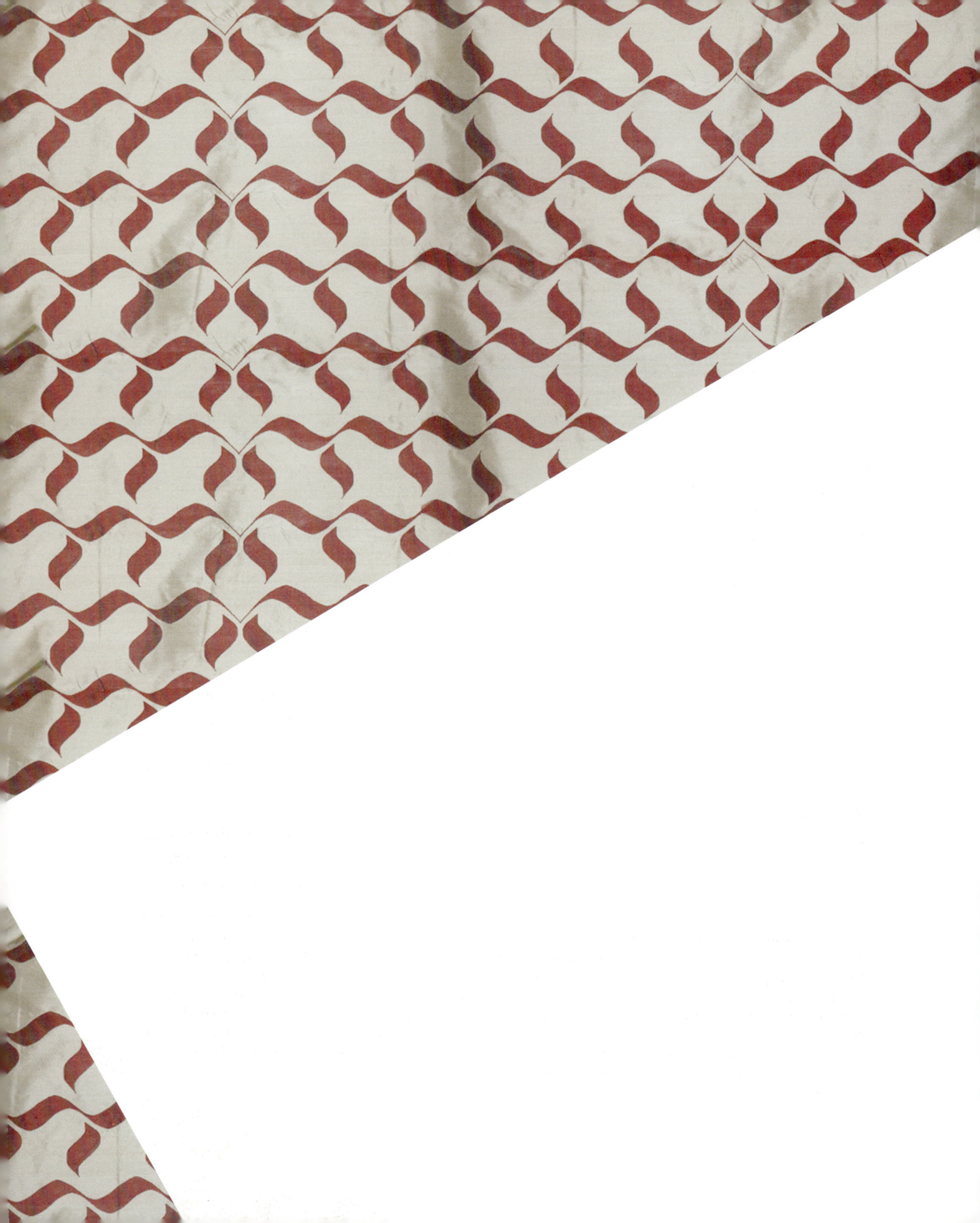

REVERENTIAL ARTWORDS

Sushma K. Bahl

The legacy of finely etched script and well-versed scribes goes back to the Vedic era of ancient India, when its oral traditions were transcribed into written shastras (sacred scriptures). Beginning with historic declarations in Sanskrit on stones, then scriptures in Brahmi (ancient script), followed by mythological epics in Pali (Middle Age Indo-Aryan) on palm leaf and the Islamic tradition of calligraphy and illustrated manuscripts on textiles and paper, and finally digital graphics in a scenario of mass production. It is this evolving heritage of the written word and calligraphy as an art form that Poosapati Parameshwar Raju uses to represent pictorially revered Indian icons, mythology, and folk tales. A master calligrapher and exponent of this art form, he is proficient in Devanagari (Indian script for Sanskrit, Hindi, and other Indian languages). With just a few strokes in minimalist sign language he manages to portray a wide spectrum of icons and epics in his own distinct oeuvre.

Route & Roots

Raghu, as he is fondly known, has his roots in the Royal Poosapati dynasty of the warrior kings of Vizianagaram in Southern India who took to drawing and mural painting, specializing in temple architecture during peace time when away from the battlefield. His father was a Lt. Col. in the army who also had a doctorate. And his great grandfather and grandfather were well-versed in Shilpa Shastra (classical Indian texts that deal with rules for making sculptures, statues, and temples).

With such a mixed ancestral history the child acquired knowledge of traditions, customs, rituals, and folklore from stories that he grew up hearing. His great grandfather, who created deities in stone and metal for the temples and worked on frescos, is also credited with developing a new mix of tamarind seed paste for his work. But, despite this background, a career in the army, rather than in the arts, was being contemplated.

Sushma K. Bahl MBE is an independent arts adviser, writer, and curator of cultural projects, based in Delhi. She is the author of 5000 Years of Indian Art, and former head of the Arts and Culture, British Council, India. Amongst other projects Bahl was the guest director for XI Triennale-India 2005, the project consultant for Bharat Rang Mahotsav X11, and jury member for the 14th Asian Art Biennale Bangladesh 2010, and the curator of India-ASEAN artists' residency and exhibition in 2012. Ways of Seeing won her the best-curated group show IHC Art India Award. Bahl is both editor and contributor for catalogs and artists' books, including those on Thota Vaikuntam, Paresh Maity, Satish Gupta, Sarla Chandra, and Shuvaprasanna. She is also a trustee and advisory board member of cultural institutions both in India and abroad.

However, an accidental slip from a mountain cliff while trekking in the Himalayas resulted in a change of course. Though fortunate to survive the accident, he could no longer join the army.

Turning full circle to his roots in the art domain, a journey through the caves of Ajanta and Ellora with his grandfather, Raghava Raju, gave the lad a good grounding in the traditional Indian grid system, enhancing his appreciation of the designs and aesthetics of artisans who created those masterpieces eons ago. For someone who was good at sketching, and loved it too, further support came from his teacher at the school in Amravatinagar, who taught him how to draw and simplify things. He also encouraged Parameshwar to join the art school from which he later graduated. The young man followed it up with post-graduate studies in applied art and design that gave him a solid foundation in techniques and visualization. As an eager apprentice he also learnt Devanagari typography and the art of pothi writing (creating traditional handmade books), besides drawing and painting from Prof S.V. Pendse. Prof B.V. Lokhande taught him the finer points of design. The three important lessons that Parameshwar, as an erudite art student, acquired from his studies – how to simplify the image, the art of scripting, and what and how to see and design – have served him well. These assets, coupled with his exposure to pan-Indian cultural practices (thanks to his extensive travels and wide ranging experiences) have shaped the course of his artistic journey, inundating it with folklore and stories about temples, gods, and idols.

The years immediately following his college studies saw the tall, soft-spoken, gentleman-artist take a detour into the corporate world to make a living, while continuing to practice calligraphy in his spare time. A series of designing jobs, including work with the Central Silk Board, the Government of Karnataka in Bangalore, advertising companies in Ahmedabad and Hyderabad (where he finally shifted to join his wife, a practicing doctor) all left their imprint on his art and aesthetics.

Parameshwar's career has also included stints teaching at the Art School in Aurangabad, CAVA in Mysore, and Chitrakala Parishath in Bangalore. The experience he had setting up a foundation and art gallery for a company in Hyderabad, his cumulative expertise in designing and packaging, and his commitment to preserving the country's cultural heritage were all triggers behind his setting up his own Foundation for Fine Arts and Crafts that took root a few years ago. The artist creates prototypes, designs utilitarian objects, documents their history, facilitates research, and collaborates with craft practitioners through the Foundation. While working on these myriad strands, he also keeps focused on creating calligraphic paintings.

Art & Aesthetics

Immersed in artistically inscribed text, letters, alphabets, markings, and words Parameshwar's art and aesthetics revolve around the spiritual and religious as they traverse through the traditional and contemporary terrains. They reflect his passion for history and documentation, knowledge of rituals and folklore, and his fine hand and technical expertise. Inspired by his training in mythology, his creative outpourings are colored by his travels and study of the Vedas (ancient Indian texts). His finely rendered alphabets are inundated with symbols, narratives, and signs – essentially reverential in ethos. They depict and rewrite the great epics, and feature iconography and avatars with their attributes and emblems. Countless gods and deities in diverse stylization and distinct scripts of different languages are re-presented in the art-scape.

Essentially based on the tradition of writing with a kalam (a reed pen dipped in ink used for inscribing), these artistic expressions are a celebration of the art of hand-written words. Loaded with pictorial possibilities for reverence and enlightenment, the work explores the beauty and power of calligraphy. The selection and construction of each character is carefully conceptualized before its formation and composition. Taking the indigenous art and craft practices into its fold, the scripted manifestations and their constituent elements are elucidated with a fervor that endows the iconography with sanctity. In a minimalist, almost abstract, oeuvre it is a visualization of the intimate relationship between image and idea.

Though adept at Devanagari script and expert in presenting its alphabets in amazingly inked art, Parameshwar makes no claims to a command of Hindi or its grammar. It is his mastery in drawing the characters in a juxtaposition of the simple and curvaceous that bequeaths his work its lyrical beauty. The various signifiers and emblems associated with different rituals and narratives that are featured alongside the alphabets penned in red ink and flanked by white blank spaces make the compositions come alive and add to their meaning and appearance. The renditions are abstract and compact. The alphabets and symbols are carefully selected to convey a deep meaning. The spectrum of Parameshwar's repertoire is extensive. Scenes feature classical Hindu epics, much-revered icons, symbols of Om (sacred utterance or mantra), and deities such as the elephant-headed God Ganesha. They also include images from other faiths – Christianity, Buddhism, Islam, and more – the art-scape extends to encompass them all. And the experimentations traverse beyond the word and calligraphic art to include working on designs for traditional folk arts and crafts and their documentation.

Mode & Material

The artist uses various tools and a range of pens and nibs, some thick and others thin, to compose his alphabets, turning them into works of fine art. A voracious reader, he studies epics, books on religion and mythology, and visits historical sites to check facts and get things right. Research precedes conceptualization and planning. Compositions are outlined on graph sheets in miniature calligraphic format. The strokes are then executed meticulously with nibs of varying thickness dipped in colored inks. The markings and letters, painstakingly etched in a mix and match of simple and curvaceous lines, create the desired image. The delicate and soft strokes are contrasted with bold and dominating ones, the space filled in with shades of reds is offset against blank areas in pure white to suggest relationships between

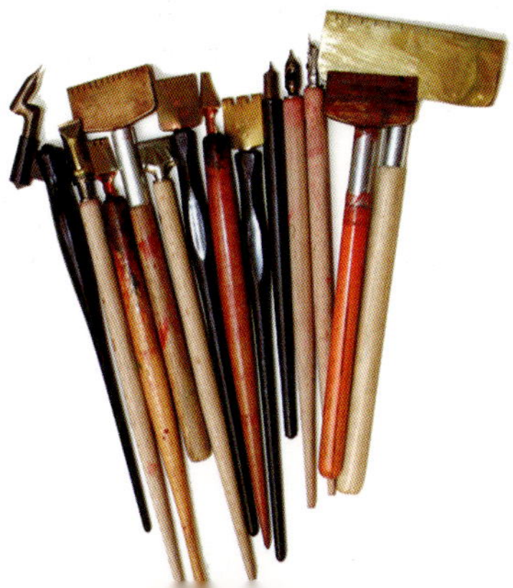

different characters and forms, as appropriate. In the Indian classical grid system a dot is placed at the center which, when divided, represents the five basic elements that make up the universe. And this is also at the crux of Parameshwar's artistic philosophy. When the expanded dot denoting Shakti (the personification of the divine feminine) is modified into a triangle it denotes Shiva as a primary godly form. The collection pulsates with a range of meticulously designed grid and space arrangements. Balance and symmetry between the empty space and the subject is carefully maintained with no overcrowding in the works. With no portraits or figures, and no background fill-ins, in simple lines and calligraphic signs, the suggestions and impressions the images evoke, spur the viewer to exercise the imagination and extract a personal meaning from each piece.

Parameshwar's studio looks busy with easels, inks, pens, a laptop, digital SLR camera, and, of course, paper and note books in various sizes neatly arranged. Missing are the regular paints and brushes. A master in Devanagari script, Parameshwar also employs English and Urdu typography. Using the central dot as the pivot, he gradually works around it to weave the magic of his spiritual leanings and artistic training. Certain characters are drawn in a horizontal vein others with a left or right slant of the stylus to build contrast. And drawing the images in pictorial calligraphic idiom, some with straight nibs and others with slanted ones, and using nibs of various thicknesses, at first the process appears somewhat tentative, but gradually the strokes transform into amazing artworks.

The work is inundated with various shades and tones of red, "a color you can't go wrong with, given its characteristic wave lengths", says the artist who often works with crimson and scarlet and admits to his fascination for the palette. The use of brown and beige in varied tints and tones are also applied to highlight shifts from dark to light – a chance discovery the artist made while working on his tree series.

Blending the old and the new – the temple art coded in calligraphy; the mixing of techniques learnt from his grandfather; his multifarious training, experiences and experimentations – the artist takes to the final paper only after he is sure of the workability of his ideas. Particular about the quality of material, he works on archival paper in a range of sizes – Canson and Bockingford 300gsm paper commonly used for watercolors is his preferred choice. Since the bright tones of normal photo color inks start to fade away within months, he takes care to use only special lightproof ink known to survive for over 100 years. He also prefers lighter and thinner colored inks. Most pieces come in editions of five, though different elements are added to each to make each one unique. The finely inscribed simple forms, alphabets, and letters imbued with meaning and symbolic value retell countless stories requiring no additional ornamentation.

The artist works in two different sessions in the morning and evening, with music playing in the background. Often two or more series run simultaneously as he shifts his focus from one to the other mulling things over. It is his use of the nib, and the pressure that he applies to the strokes in carefully measured tones, that define his rigor and expertise. The space division and grid planning are central to the design of his compositions in which graphics and alphabets are inscribed in a manner similar to pothi writing – which involved inscribing palm leaves with a stylus in a bygone era. It also echoes some of the features of illustrated manuscripts, but without the ornamentation.

It is Parameshwar's experimentation with different materials and rigorous practices that have helped him perfect his techniques in creating such poignant imagery. While it takes him three to four months to plan a work, it might take him just a few hours or days to finally execute it. Some works take longer than the others. Though an average work is drawn and painted in 3 to 4 layers, some need up to ten layers. The top layer of thin lines dries fast, with each subsequent layer taking longer to mature with the thicker layers helping to achieve variable textures. Nibs of different thicknesses are used to convey specific ideas and draw diverse types of letters and forms.

The basic layout is conceived in small size with English poster nibs filled with ink, while the final image is worked on with larger nibs dipped into ink. Standing up and holding the nib down, pressure is applied to get the colors into the surface. The image is inlaid onto the paper, held by hand as it is moved around in various positions according to the demands of the composition. Wet tissues are used to keep hands clean and ensure the white spaces do not get spoilt or soiled. A range of pens and nibs of various thicknesses and makes are used.

With just a very few simple and measured strokes of colored ink, he is able to bring alive scenes featuring Hindu deities such as the wedding of Rama and Sita, Vishnu on Garuda, and episodes from Shiva Purana. The rhythmic formations evoke icons and mystique through symbols and metaphors and bring the work beyond the gallery precincts into the public domain.

Repertoire & Range

The artist's repertoire is vast, ranging from depictions of the Hindu Trinity (Brahma, Vishnu and Shiva), and other gods and deities, to legends of Krishna and Rama, stylized symbols of Om, Navagraha (nine cosmic influencers or Zodiac signs), Surya (the sun god), as well as trees and birds. The artist also collaborates with other artisans and craftsmen. His designs and packaging of creations such as temple lamps, boxes, and fabrics are unconventional and contemporary. Such creations help bridge the gap between high and low art or art and craft, and commerce and art.

This current collection is a selection of series spanning Buddhist symbols, Ek Omkar, Jewish symbols, the hundred names of Allah, Ahura Mazda, Christian symbols, epic narratives, numerical yantras (mystical symbols for astrological benefits), ayatanas (sense spheres), and the mythological epics of Ramayana and the Bhagavatam. The renditions are based on personal encounters during his numerous sojourns and studies. Specific symbols are used to convey particular ideas and images – the sacred red Bindu, or dot symbol, suggests the Goddess, while lotuses and vajras (thunderbolts) make reference to navagrahas (nine Zodiac signs).

In the Ramayana series that took seven years to complete, episodes such as performance of yagya (offerings in fire accompanied by ritual chants) are featured. King Dasaratha (in bigger and more emphatic strokes) and his three wives (with flower buds tucked in their round hairdos drawn in swift circular strokes), appear across the sacred fire (which is represented by short and wavy markings in the middle) as they receive a magic potion. Maid Manthara, with her hunched back drawn in a curved line holding a slightly bent stick, took months to materialize, as "I wanted to show her crookedness, but also her age, with grace", explains the artist. Other scenes such as Sita's swayamvara (the ancient custom of a girl choosing a husband from amongst her suitors); or Rama with Sita, Lakshman, and Hanuman; are shown in strokes, sizes and sequences commensurate with their hierarchical position.

There are several mythological episodes about Krishna. There is the scene of his stealing butter standing atop his friends (represented by tiny strokes in various shapes forming a pyramid), while three little girls are featured standing aside and watching it all in awe. There is the chirharan (Krishna's stealing the clothes of bathing maids). There is the scene where the gopis (cowherd maids), shown in curved forms, are bathing in the wavy river. Also depicted is Krishna playing the flute under a tree, as his mesmerized cows listen in enchantment.

There are similar representations of other faiths in minimal and measured strokes suggestive of their distinct symbols. While the Christmas tree and sacred heart represent Christianity, Buddhism is suggested by strokes that recall the Stupa (a semispherical structure containing Buddhist relics) and the Dharmachakra (the wheel of enlightenment). There are alphabets and lines that evoke Hamsa (a palm shaped amulet believed to protect against the evil eye) for the Jews, and Khanda (an emblem as an amalgam of three symbols of faith) for the Sikhs.

Though not included in the present collection, the artist's work with craftsmen should be mentioned. These include over a thousand designs on saris bearing calligraphic motifs of Nagadevata (the snake God) and tree of life patterns; his three dimensional designs for inlay jewelry makers, and those who make puja items in metal, wooden crystals, and stones.These works illustrate his wider creative repertoire encompassing fine art, calligraphy, and functional art. His art practices not only include skill and content matches, but also combine functional attributes with aesthetics.

Evidently, Poosapati Parameshwar Raju who is also engaged with documentation of indigenous and contemporary pictorial processes creates a world of reverential words in his art that is rooted in the 'soil' he comes from; as it also routes through contemporary techniques, trends and domains.

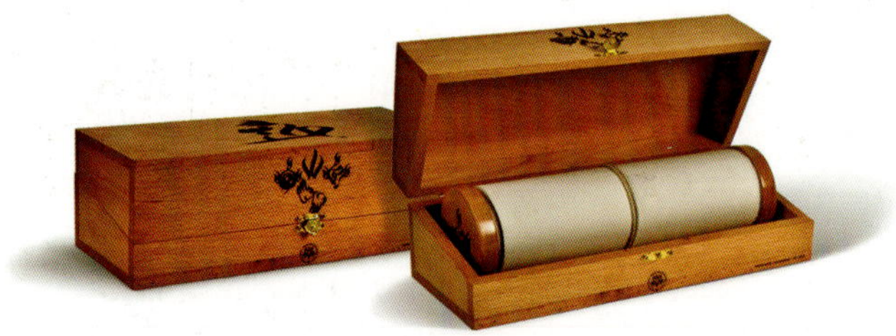

NOTE: The quotes are based on the writer's conversations with the artist.

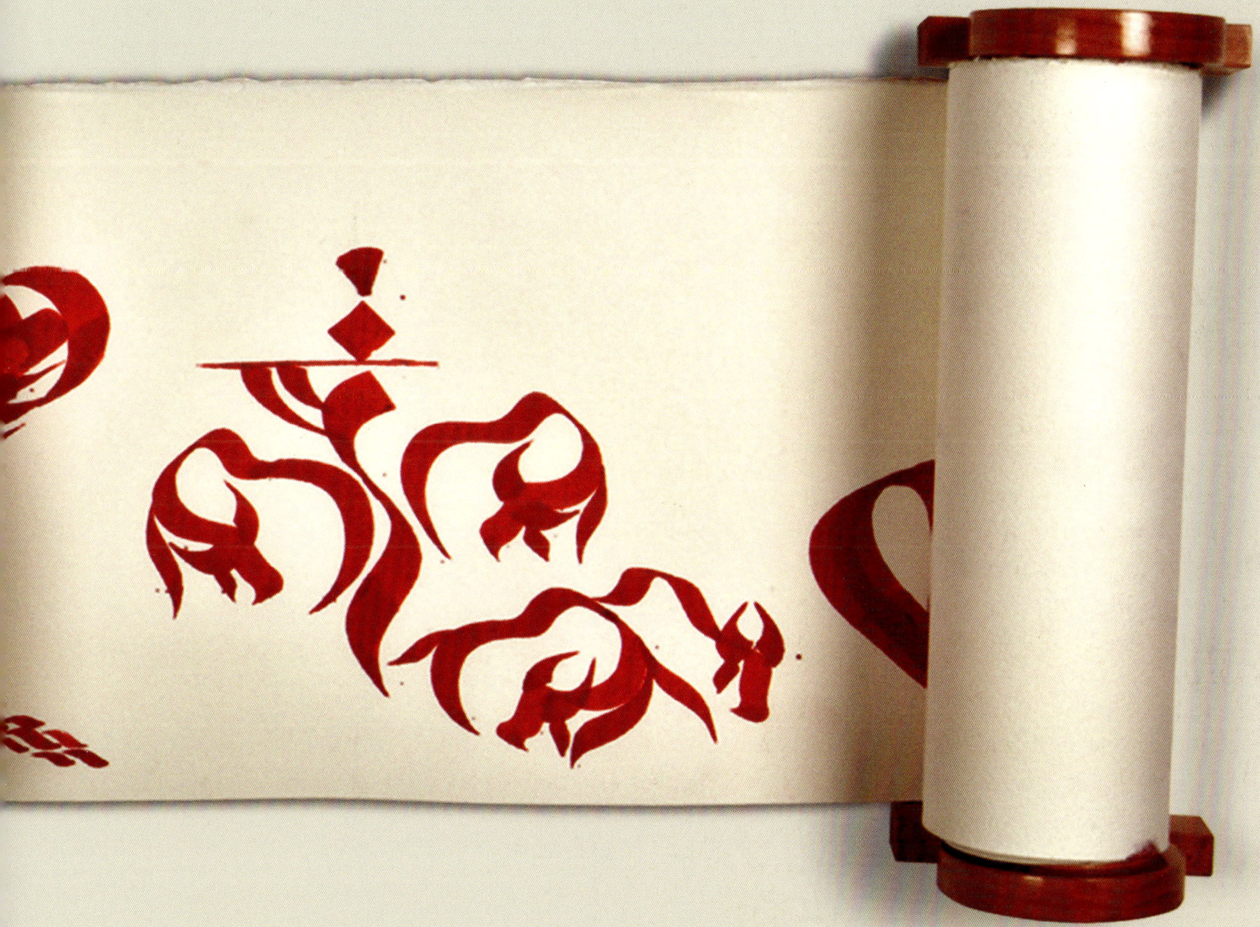

RAMAYANA

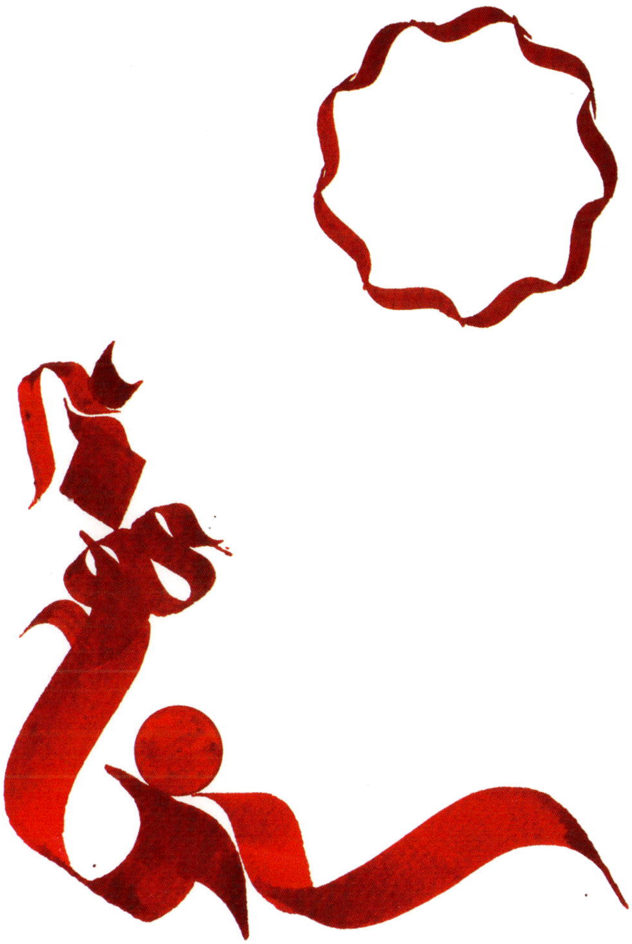

Shiva narrating the Ramayana to Parvati
Calligraphy ink on archival paper, 32 x 24 cm

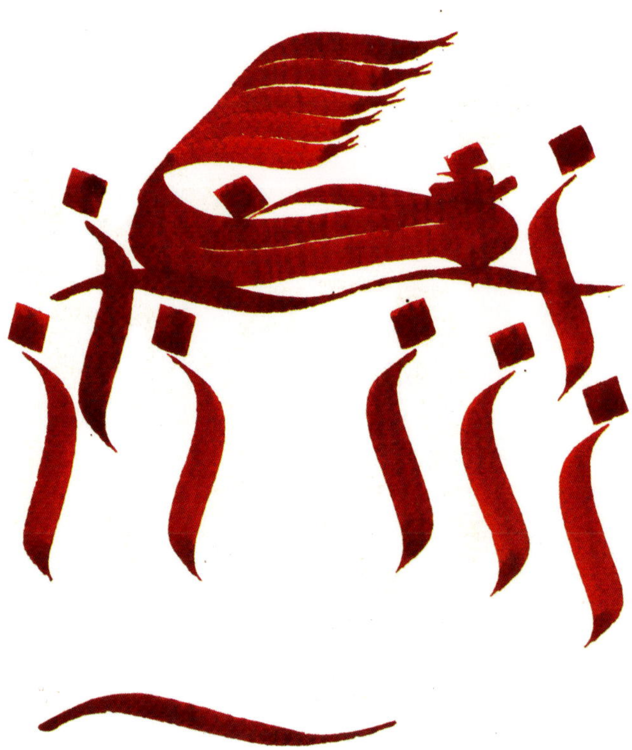

Lord Vishnu reassures the demigods He'll incarnate as Rama
Calligraphy ink on archival paper, 32 x 24 cm

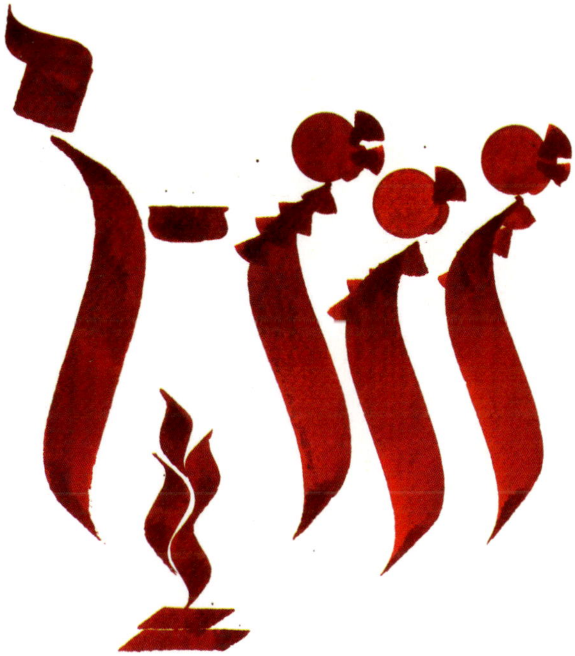

King Dasaratha and his Queens
Calligraphy ink on archival paper, 32 x 24 cm

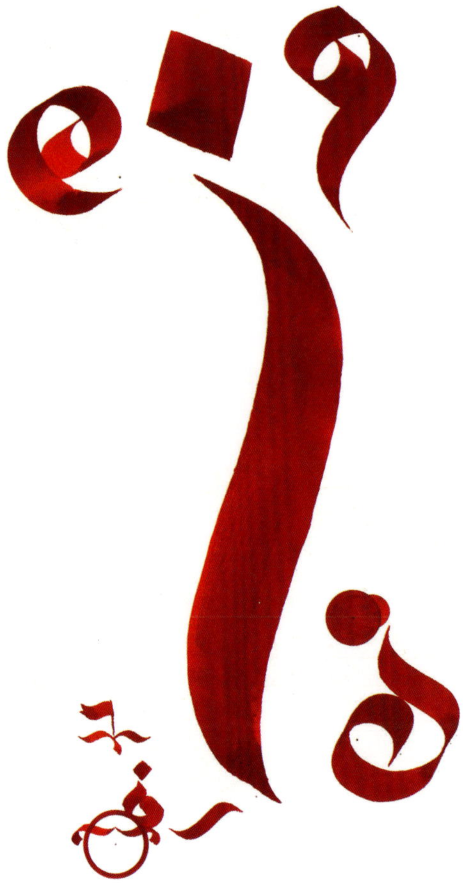

Kaushalya's Visvarupa darshan
Calligraphy ink on archival paper, 48 x 33 cm

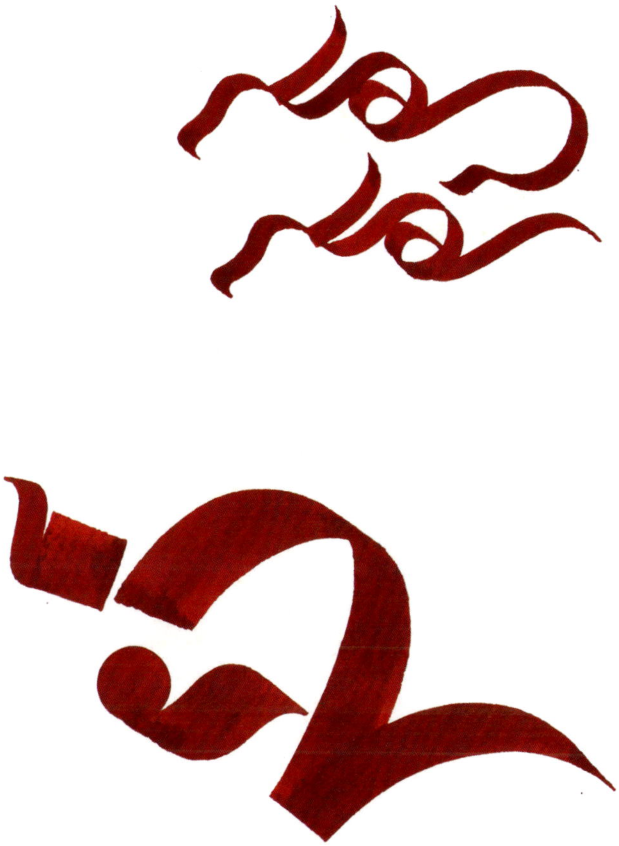

Birth of Sita
Calligraphy ink on archival paper, 32 x 24 cm

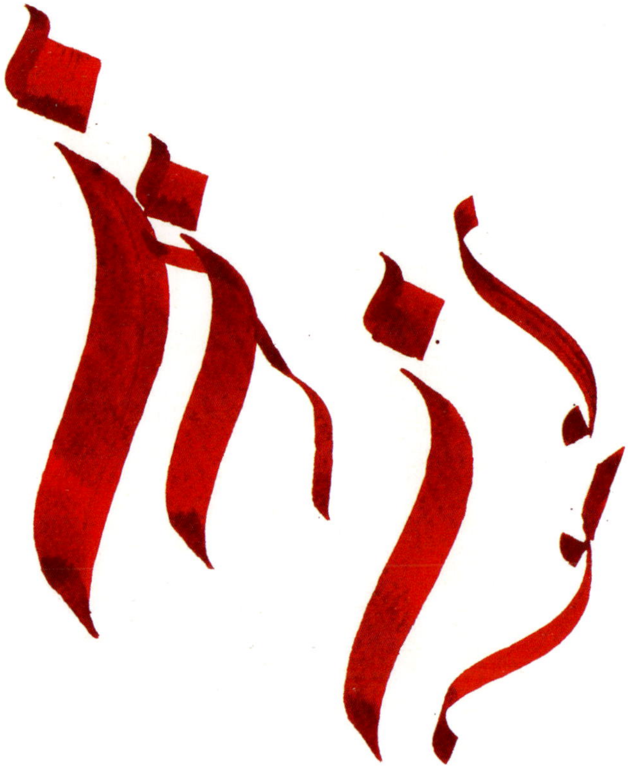

Rama strings the Hara dhanu
Calligraphy ink on archival paper, 32 x 24 cm

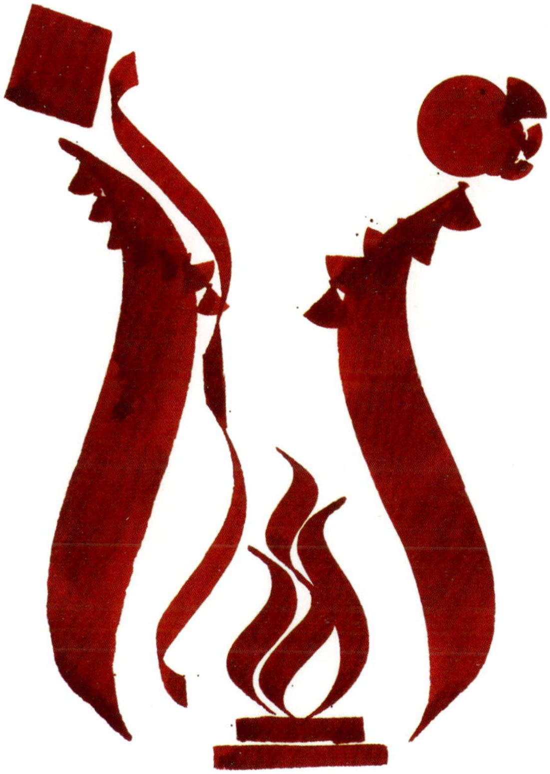

Sita Swayamvar
Calligraphy ink on archival paper, 32 x 24 cm

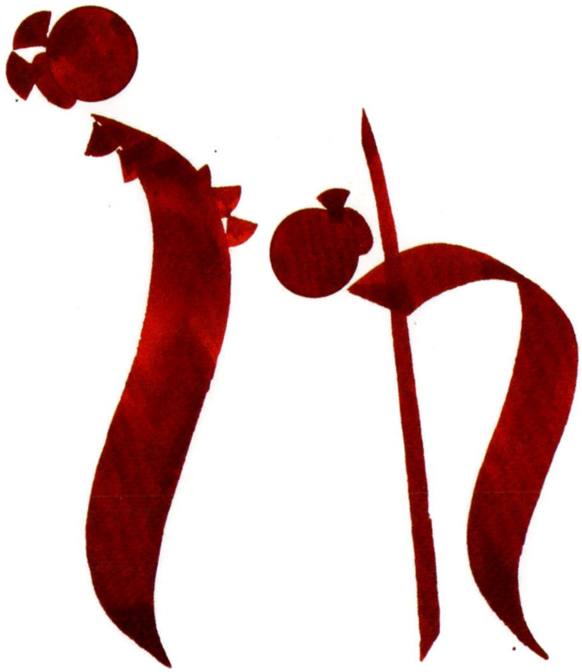

Queen Kaikeyi and Manthara
Calligraphy ink on archival paper, 32 x 24 cm

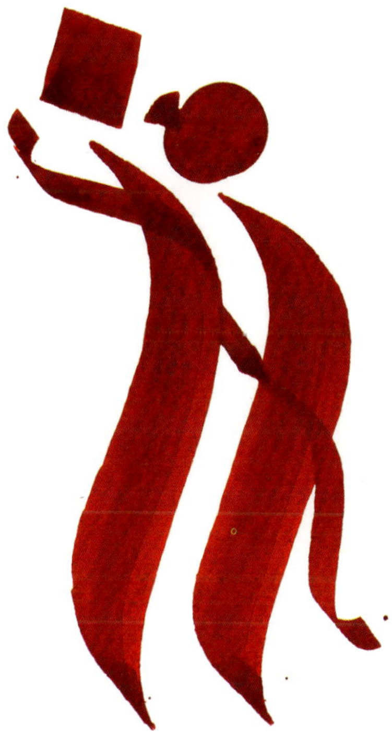

Sita decides to join Rama
Calligraphy ink on archival paper, 32 x 24 cm

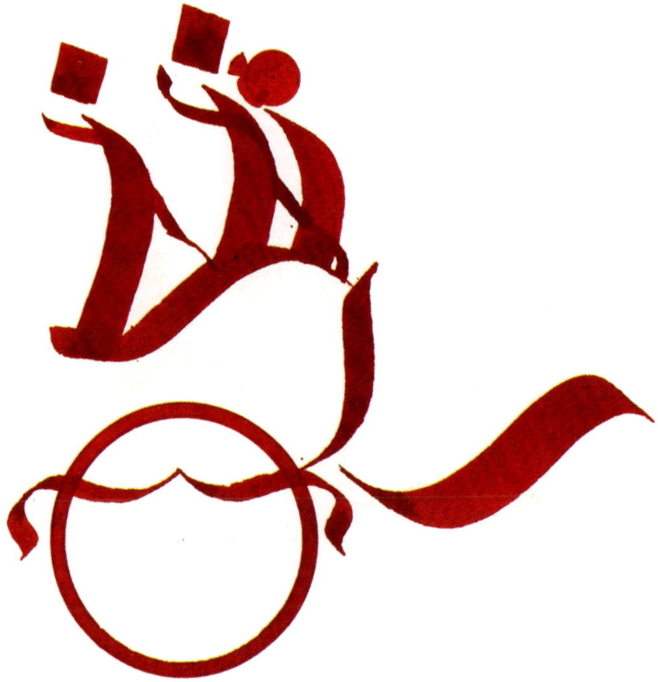

Rama, Sita, and Lakshman leave Ayodhya in a chariot
Calligraphy ink on archival paper, 32 x 24 cm

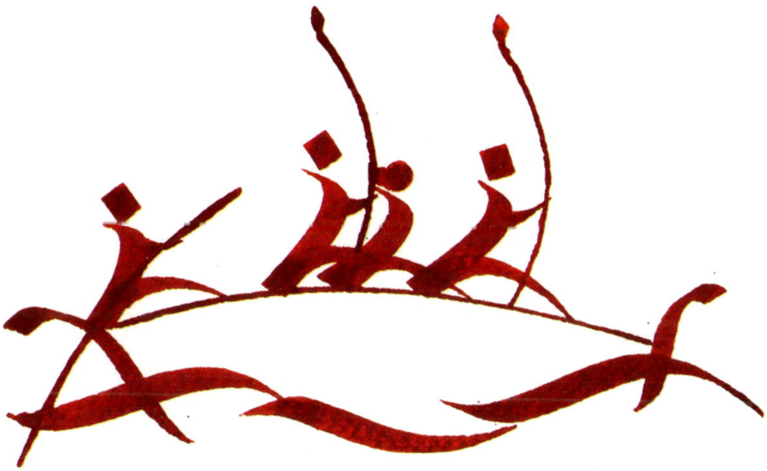

Across river Sarayu
Calligraphy ink on archival paper, 32 x 24 cm

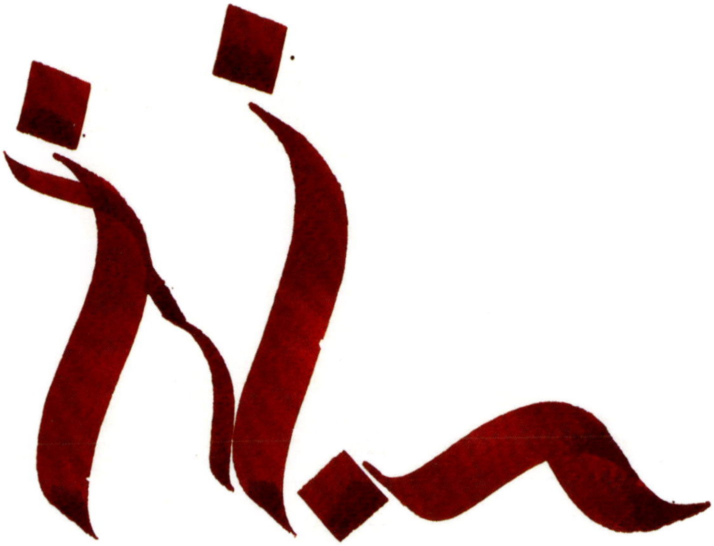

Bharata requests Rama to return to Ayodhya
Calligraphy ink on archival paper, 32 x 24 cm

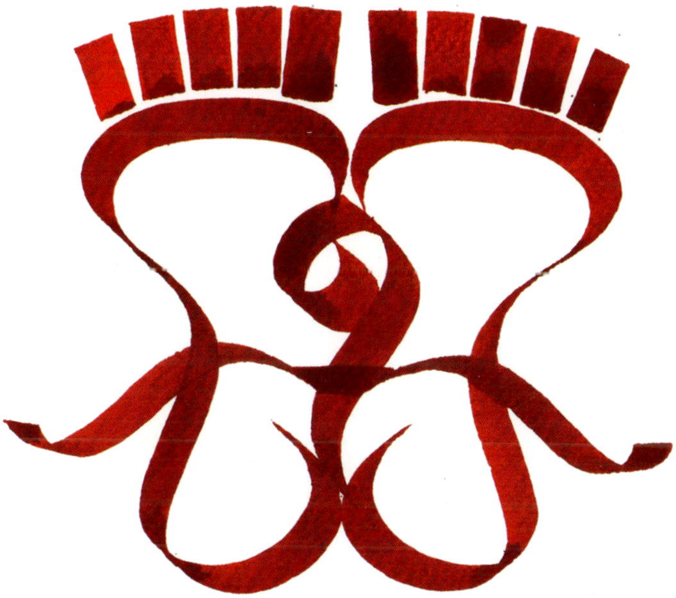

Bharata carries Rama's paduka to Ayodhya
Calligraphy ink on archival paper, 32 x 24 cm

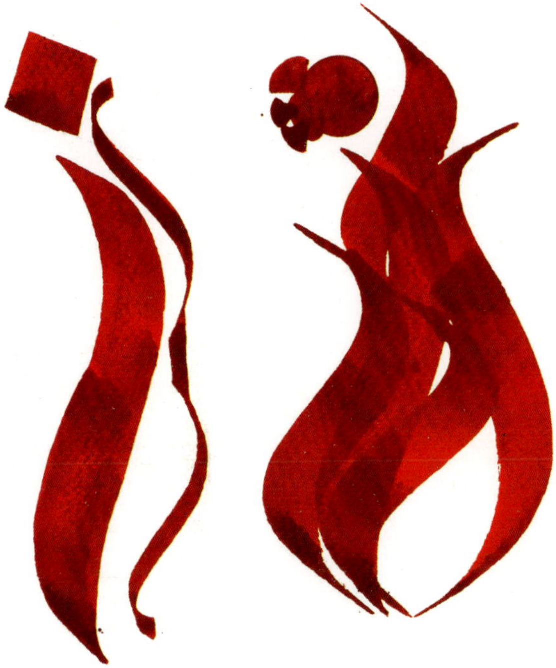

Rama protecting Sita
Calligraphy ink on archival paper, 32 x 24 cm

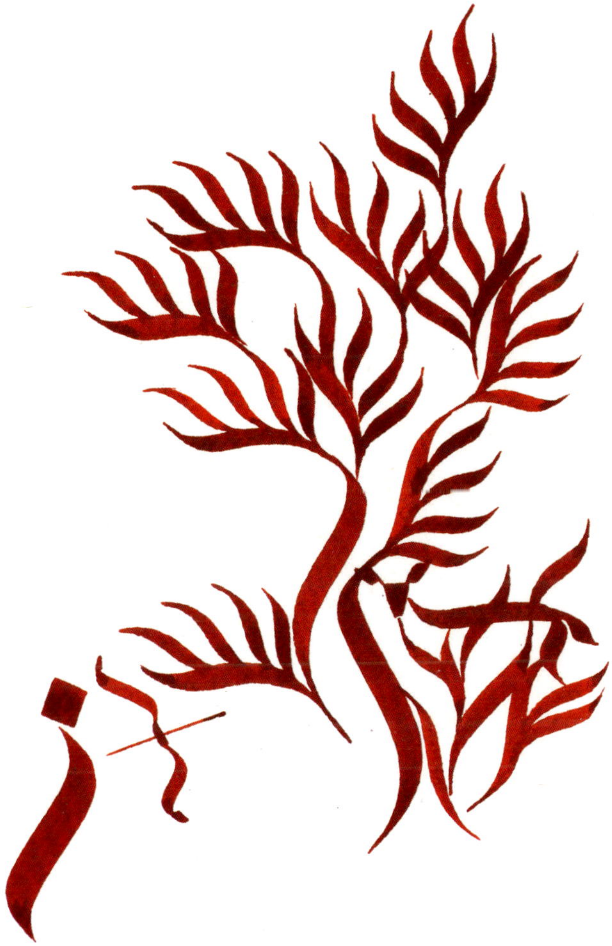

Rama aims to capture Marichi
Calligraphy ink on archival paper, 32 x 24 cm

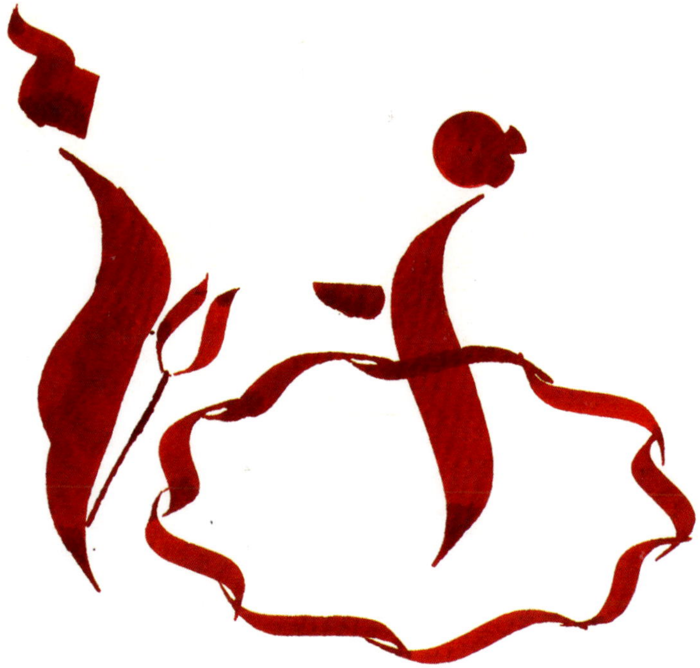

Ravana the King of Lanka
Calligraphy ink on archival paper, 32 x 24 cm

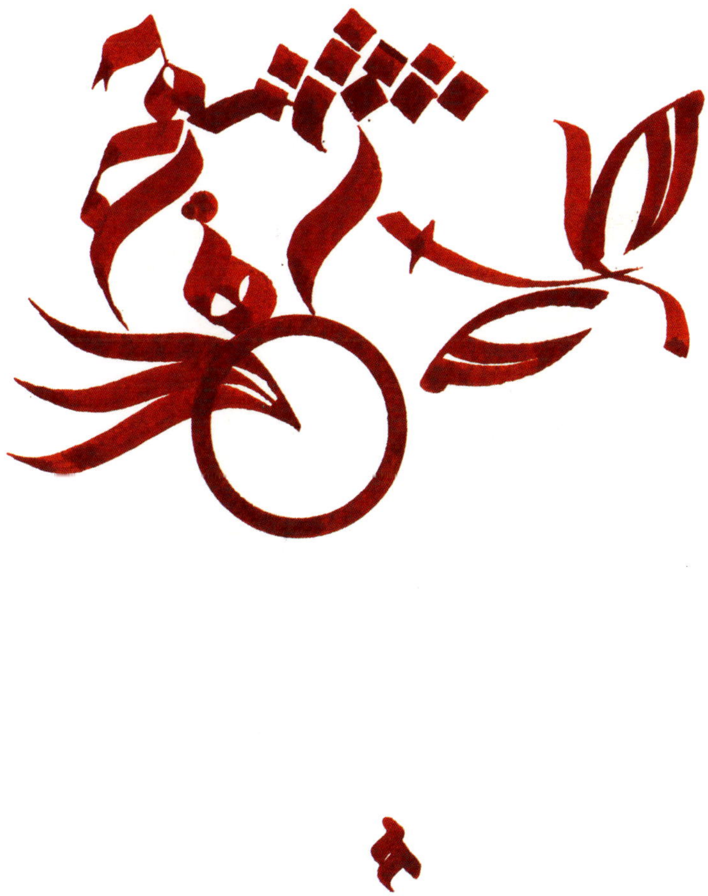

Ravana abducting Sita and confronted by Jatayu
Calligraphy ink on archival paper, 32 x 24 cm

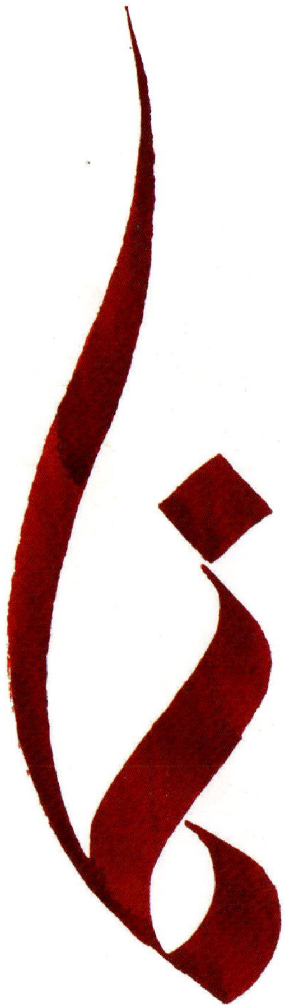

Hanuman
Calligraphy ink on archival paper, 32 x 24 cm

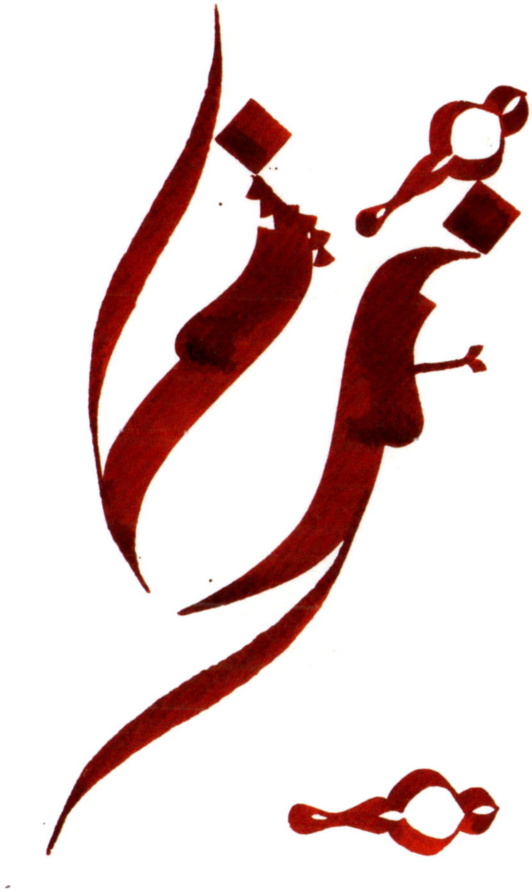

The defeat of Vali
Calligraphy ink on archival paper, 32 x 24 cm

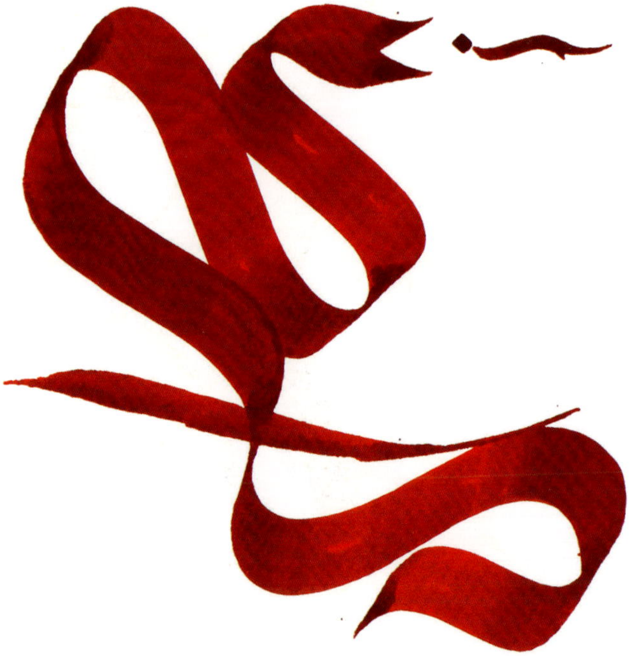

Surasa and Hanuman
Calligraphy ink on archival paper, 32 x 24 cm

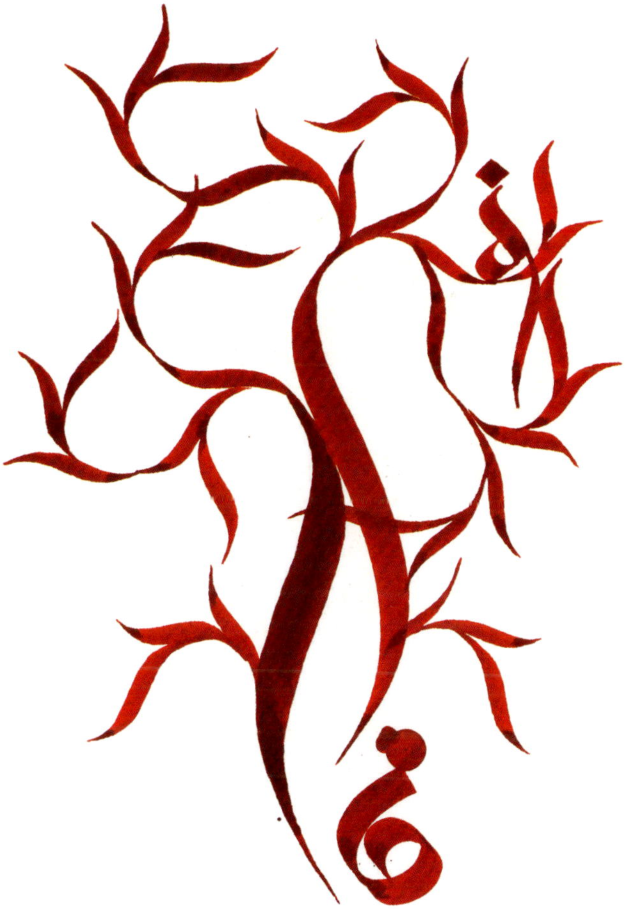

Hanuman finds Sita
Calligraphy ink on archival paper, 32 x 24 cm

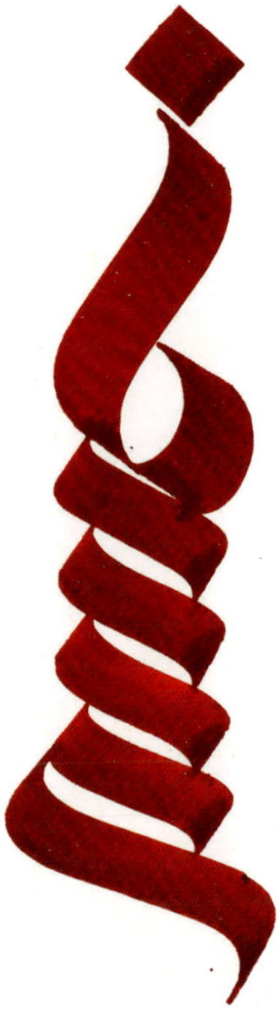

Hanuman raises himself at the court of Ravana
Calligraphy ink on archival paper, 32 x 24 cm

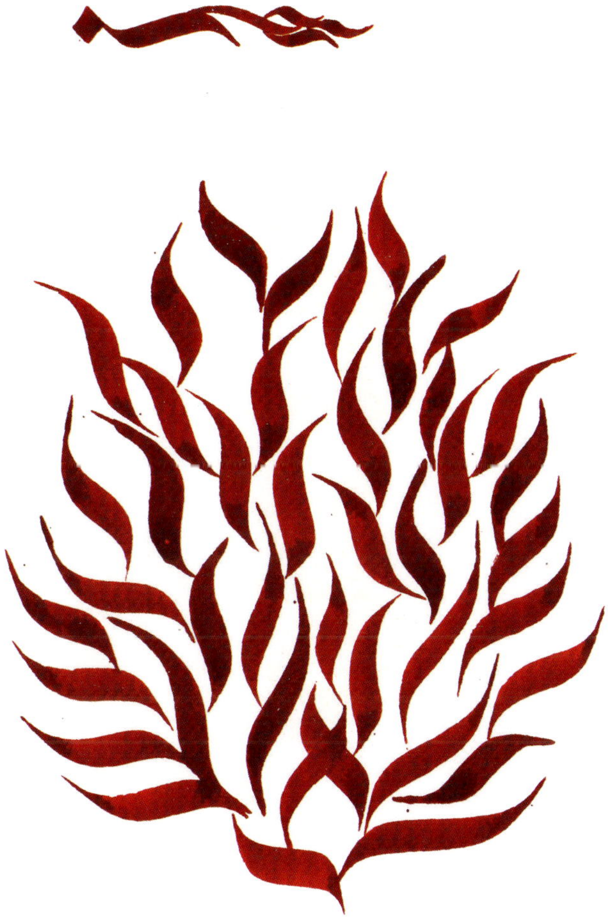

Hanuman burns Lanka
Calligraphy ink on archival paper, 32 x 24 cm

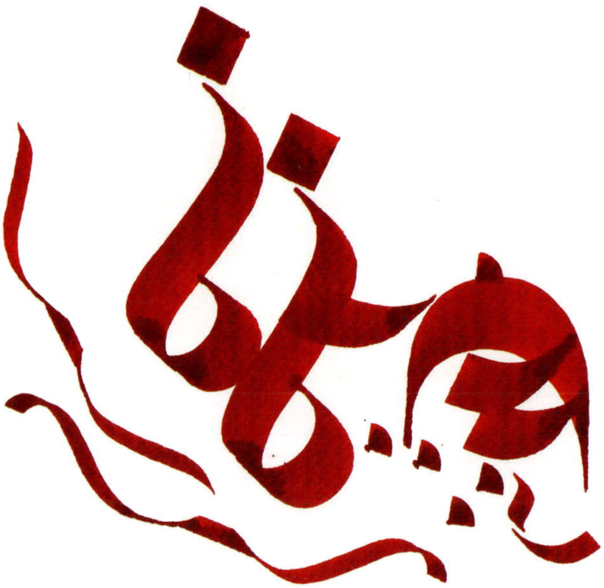

Nal and Nil
Calligraphy ink on archival paper, 32 x 24 cm

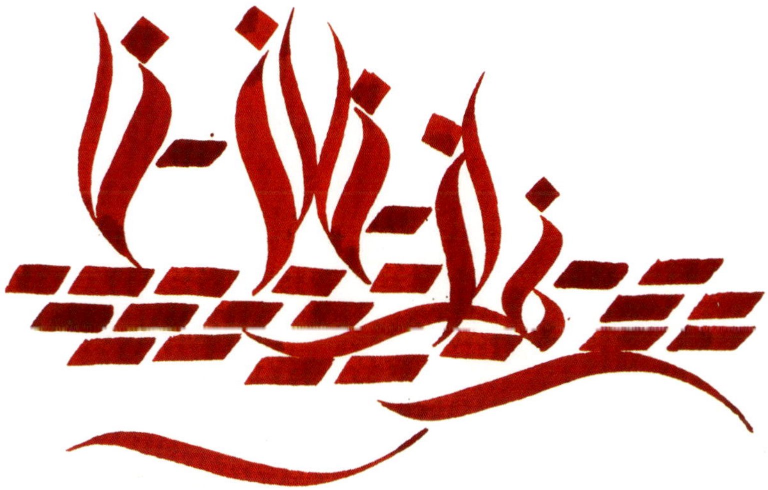

Rama and Lakshmana worship Shiva
Calligraphy ink on archival paper, 32 x 24 cm

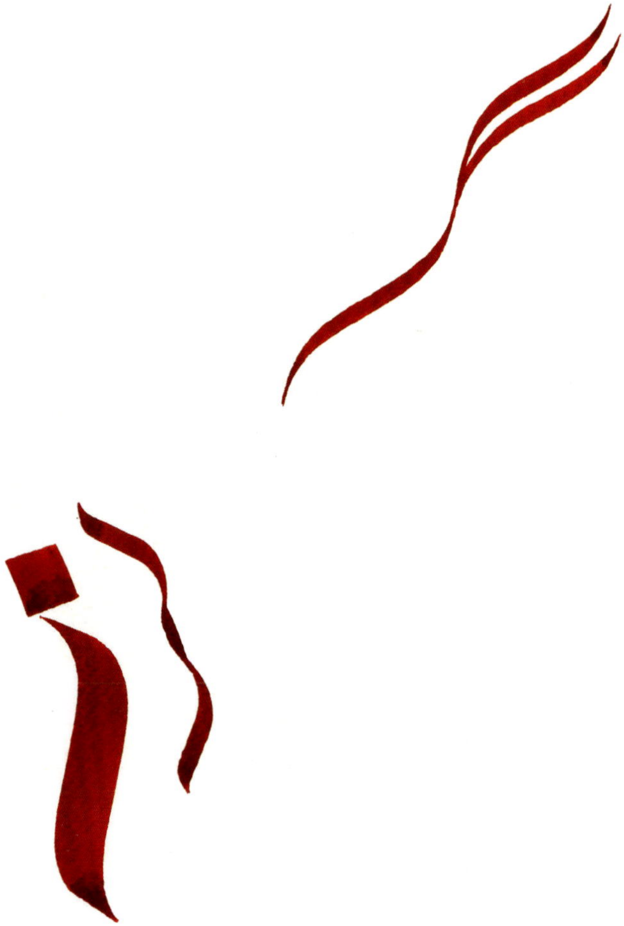

Indrajit's weapon
Calligraphy ink on archival paper, 32 x 24 cm

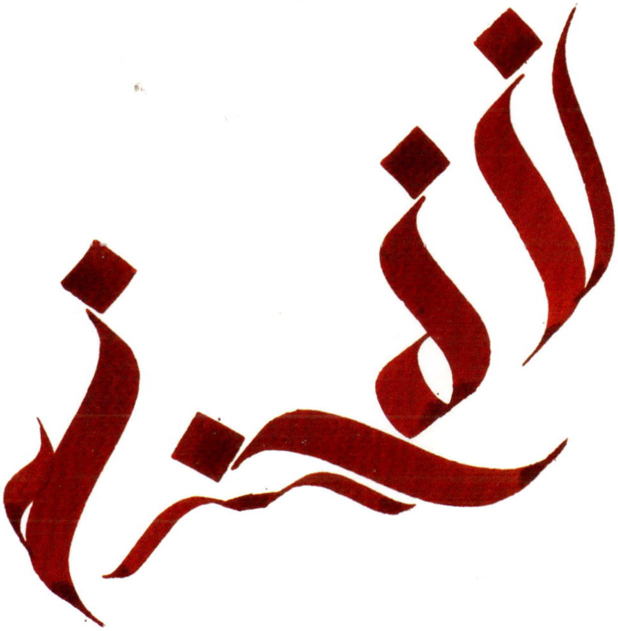

Bound by the Nagapash, Lakshmana falls unconscious
Calligraphy ink on archival paper, 32 x 24 cm

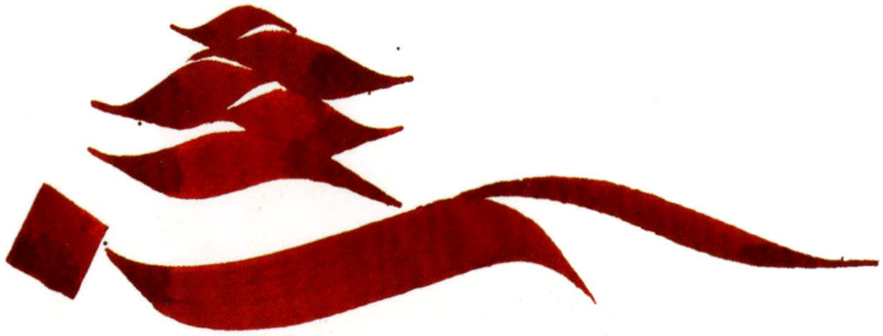

Hanuman and the Dronagiri mountain
Calligraphy ink on archival paper, 32 x 24 cm

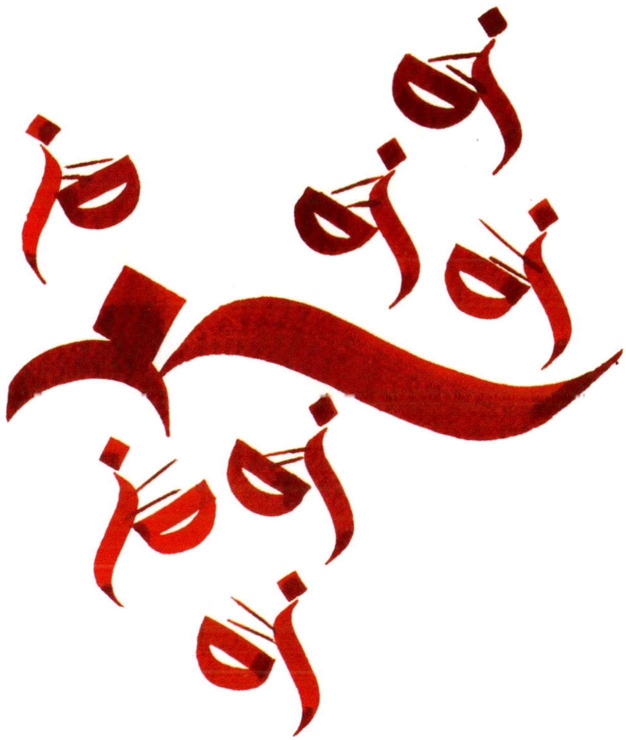

The Rakshasas playing drums
Calligraphy ink on archival paper, 32 x 24 cm

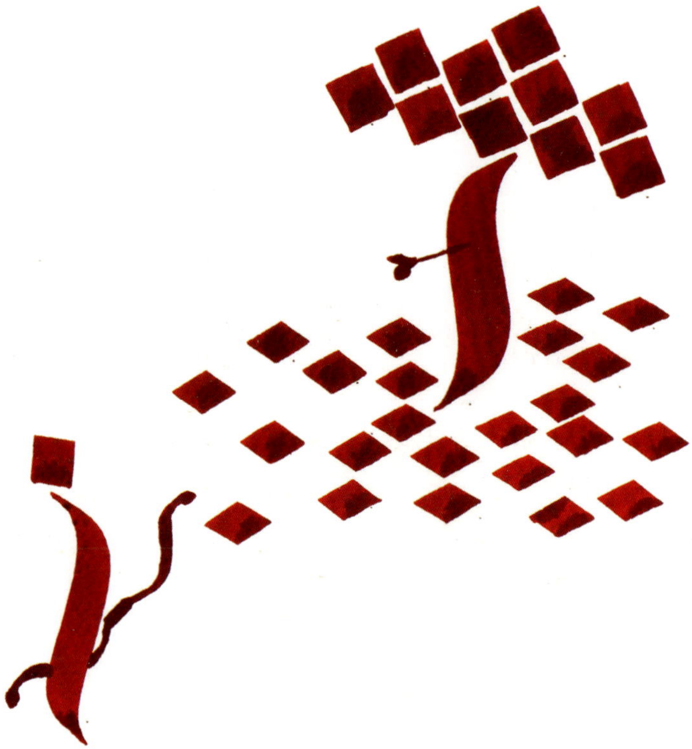

Rama defeats Ravana
Calligraphy ink on archival paper, 32 x 24 cm

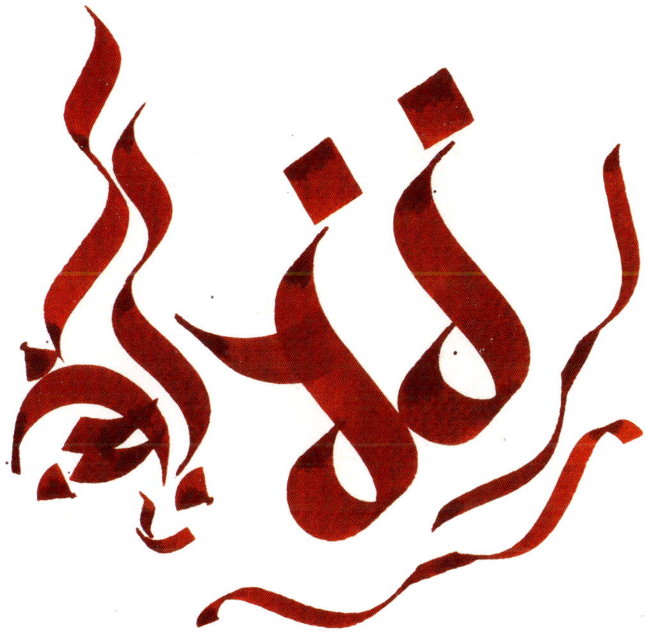

Rama and Lakshmana worship lord Shiva after the war
Calligraphy ink on archival paper, 32 x 24 cm

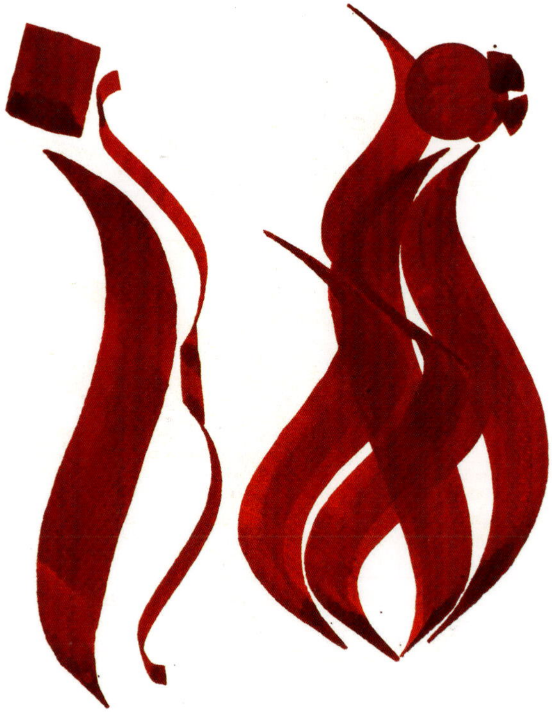

Sita comes back from the care of Agni
Calligraphy ink on archival paper, 32 x 24 cm

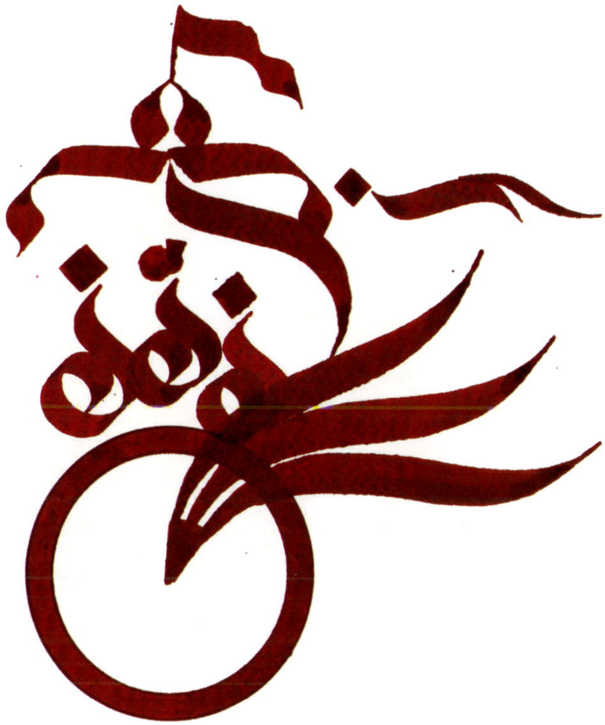

The return to Ayodhya
Calligraphy ink on archival paper, 32 x 24 cm

The festival of lights in Ayodhya
Calligraphy ink on archival paper, 32 x 24 cm

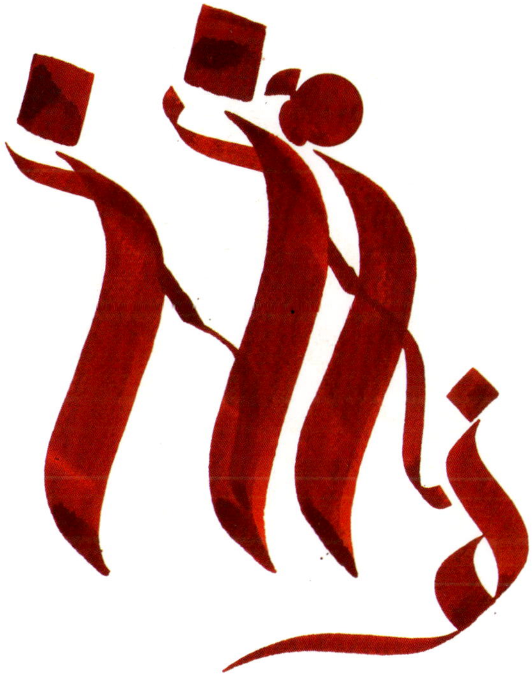

Rama, Sita, Lakshmana, and Hanuman
Calligraphy ink on archival paper, 32 x 24 cm

KRISHNA

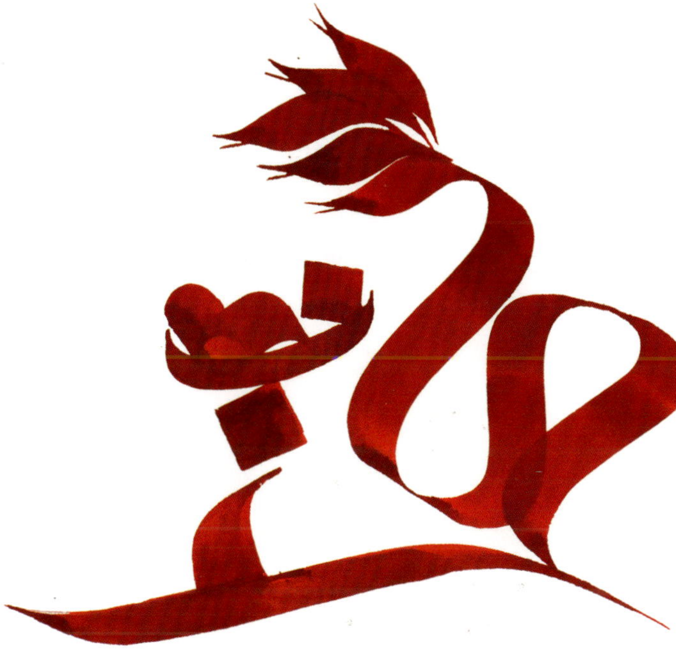

Vasudev carries the new born Krishna across the Yamuna
Calligraphy ink on archival paper, 48 x 33 cm

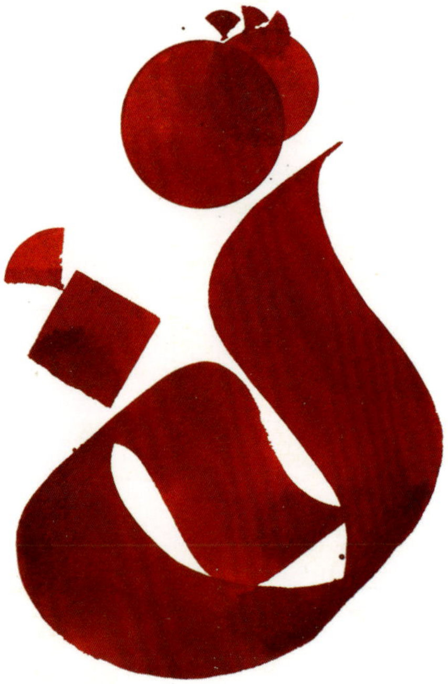

Yashoda and Krishna
Calligraphy ink on archival paper, 48 x 33 cm

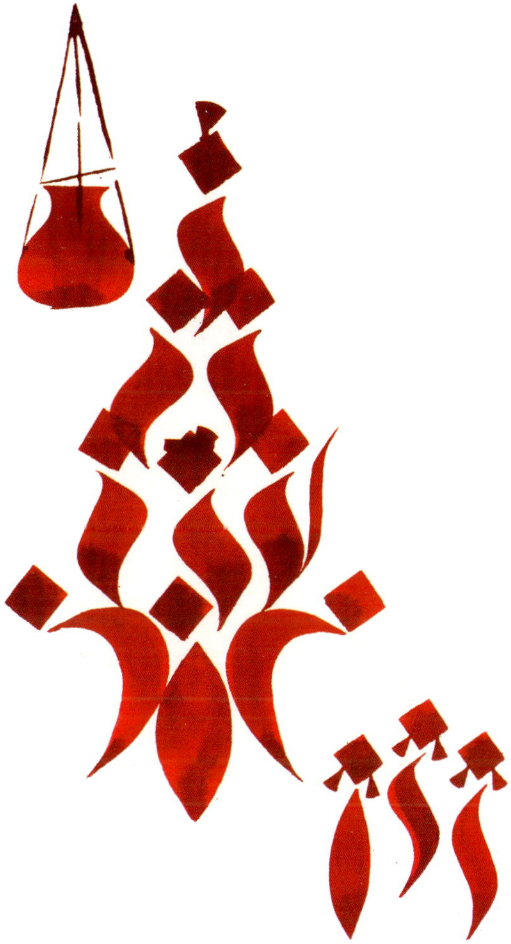

Krishna stealing butter
Calligraphy ink on archival paper, 48 x 33 cm

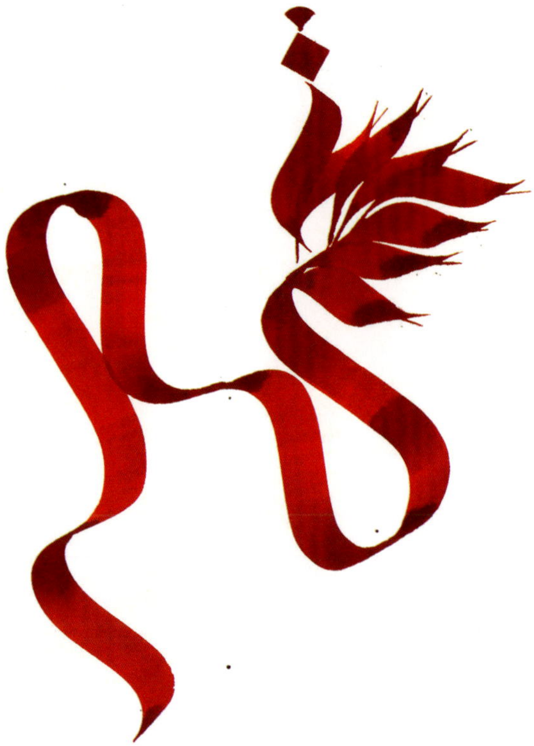

Kaliya (seven headed serpent) submits to Krishna
Calligraphy ink on archival paper, 48 x 33 cm

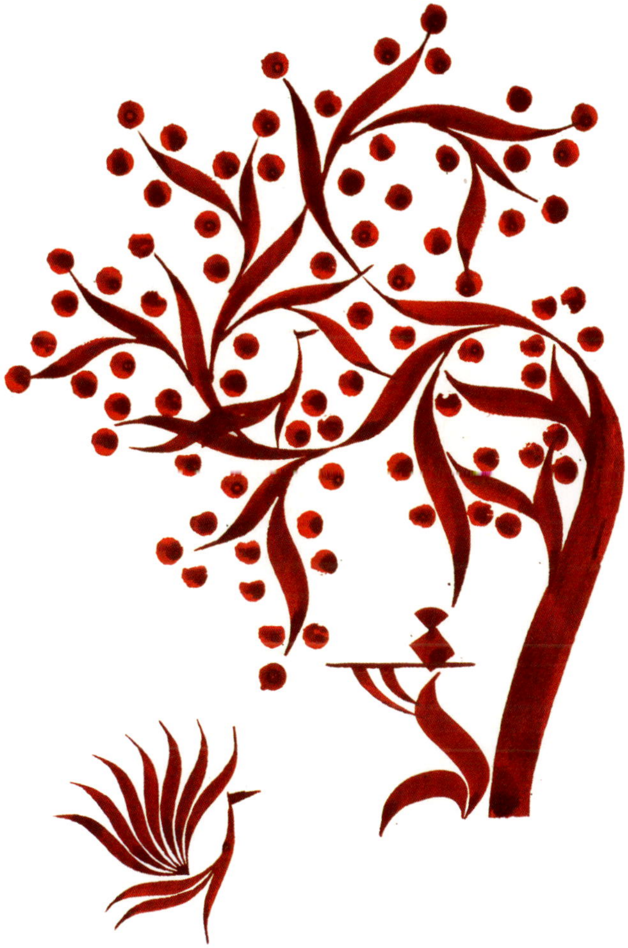

The festival of bliss
Calligraphy ink on archival paper, 42 x 30 cm

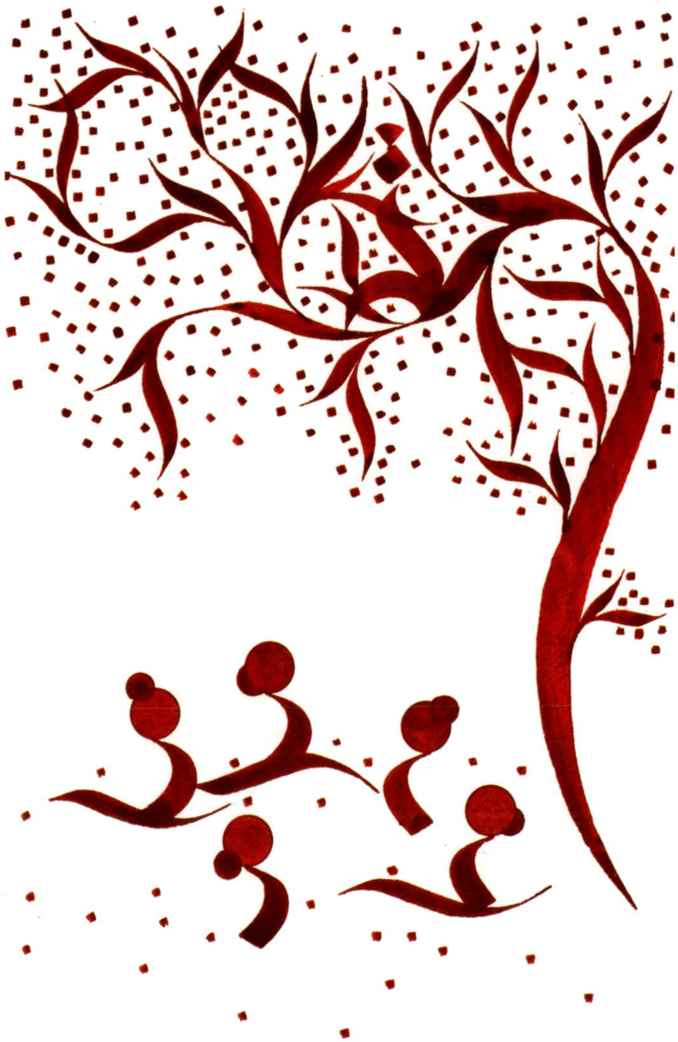

The Chir Haran Lila and the humbled Gopikas
Calligraphy ink on archival paper, 42 x3 0 cm

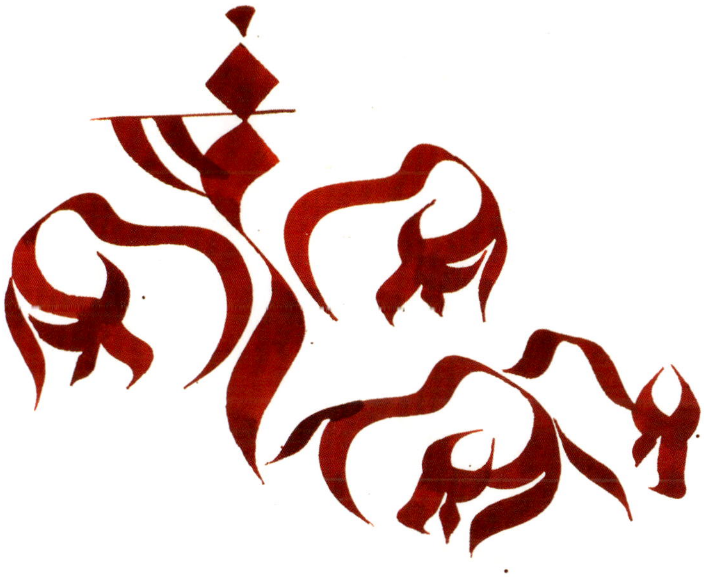

Krishna playing flute while cows graze
Calligraphy ink on archival paper, 48 x 33 cm

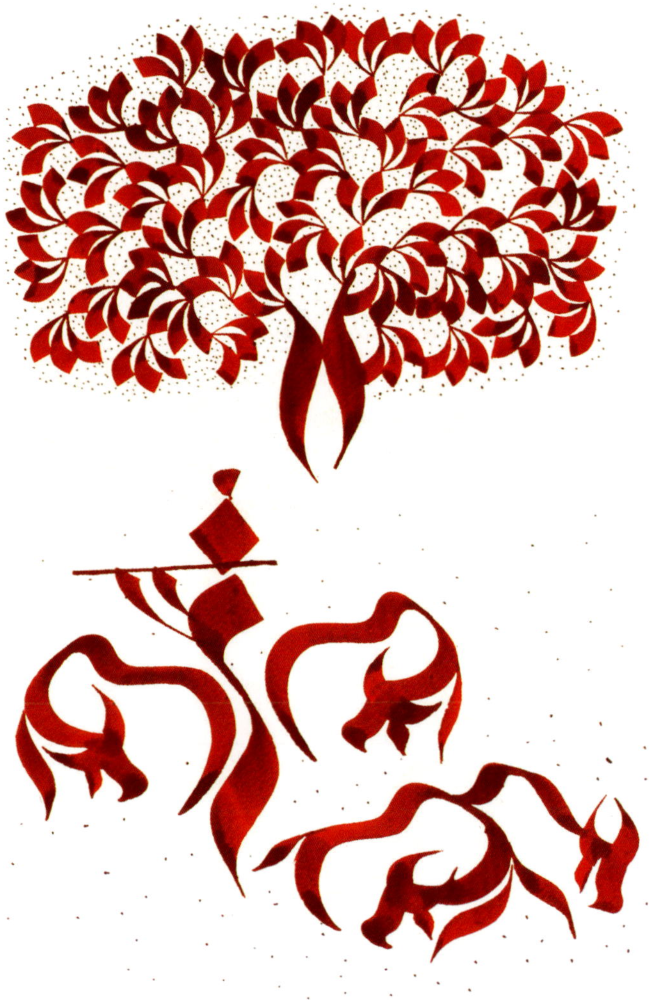

Krishna playing flute under a tree
Calligraphy ink on archival paper, 42 x 30 cm

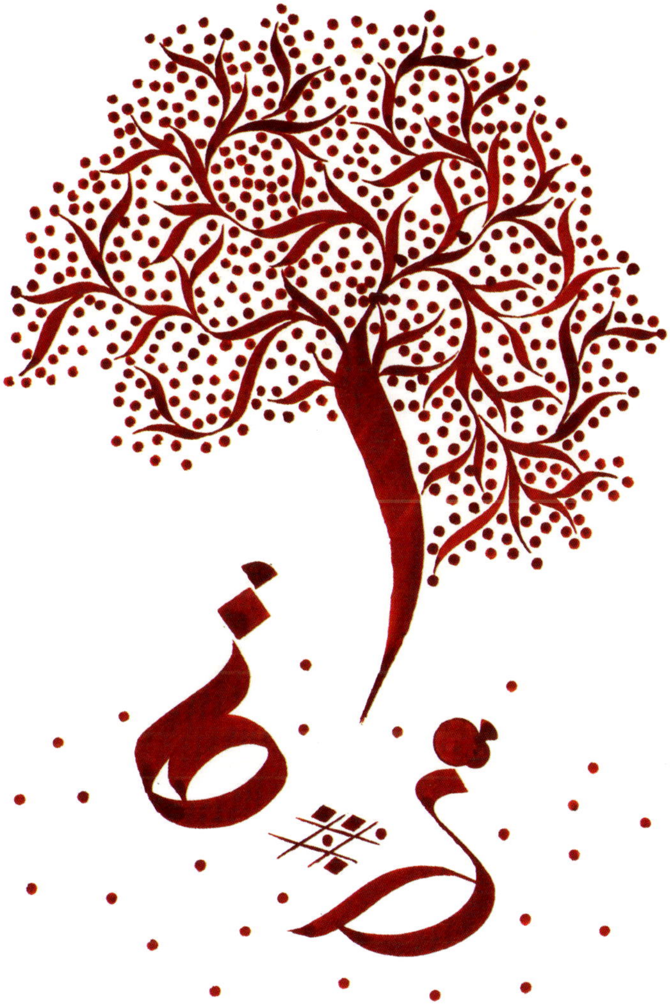

Radha-Krishna playing game under a flowering tree
Calligraphy ink on archival paper, 42 x 30 cm

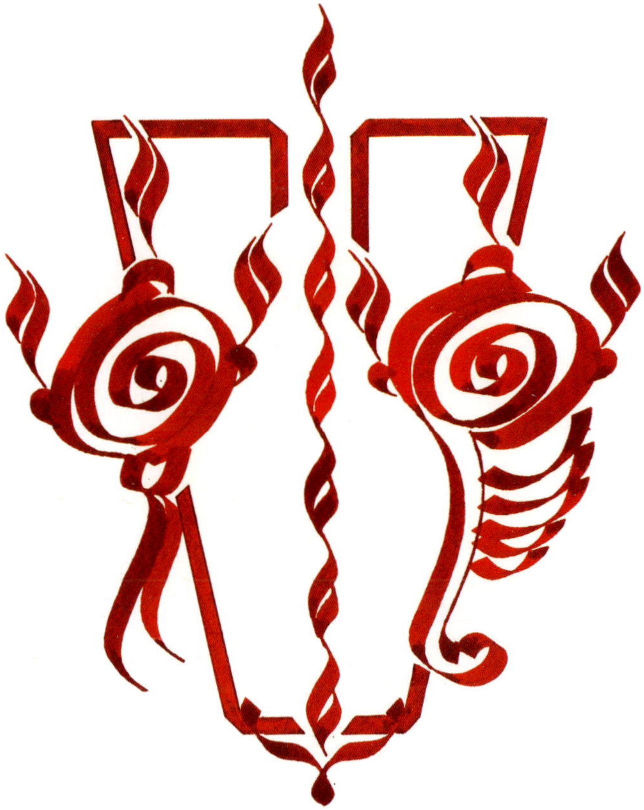

Venkateshwara Namam
Calligraphy ink on archival paper, 42 x 30 cm

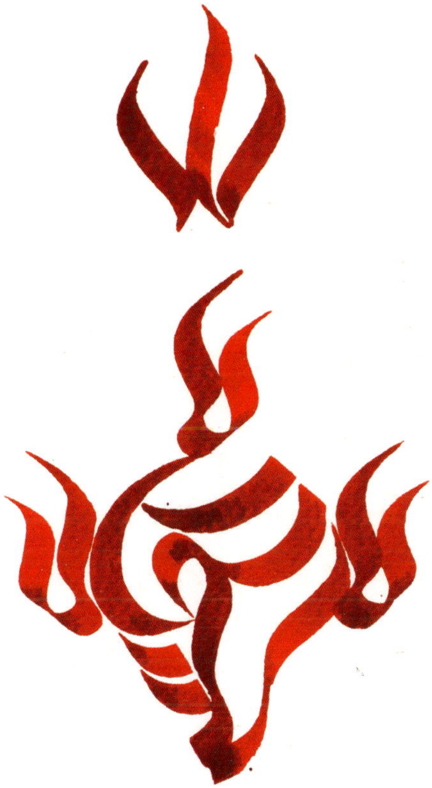

Pundarikaksha Namam and Shankh
Calligraphy ink on archival paper, 32 x 24 cm

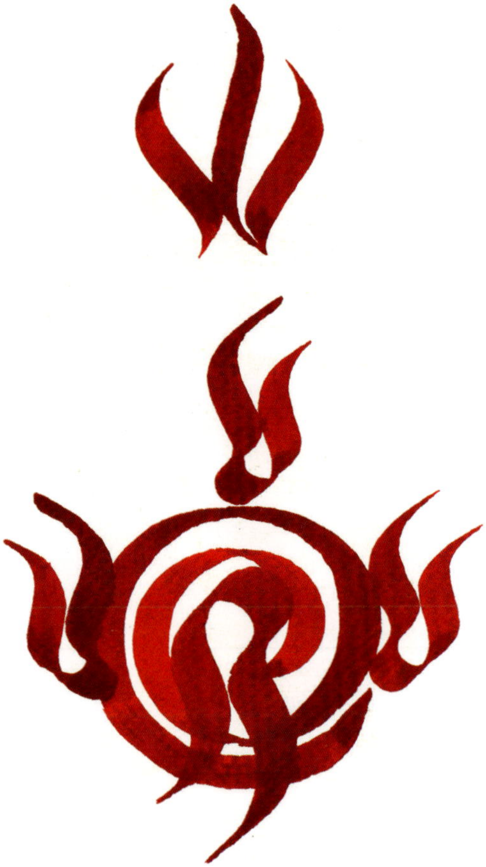

Pundarikaksha Namam and Chakra
Calligraphy ink on archival paper, 32 x 24 cm

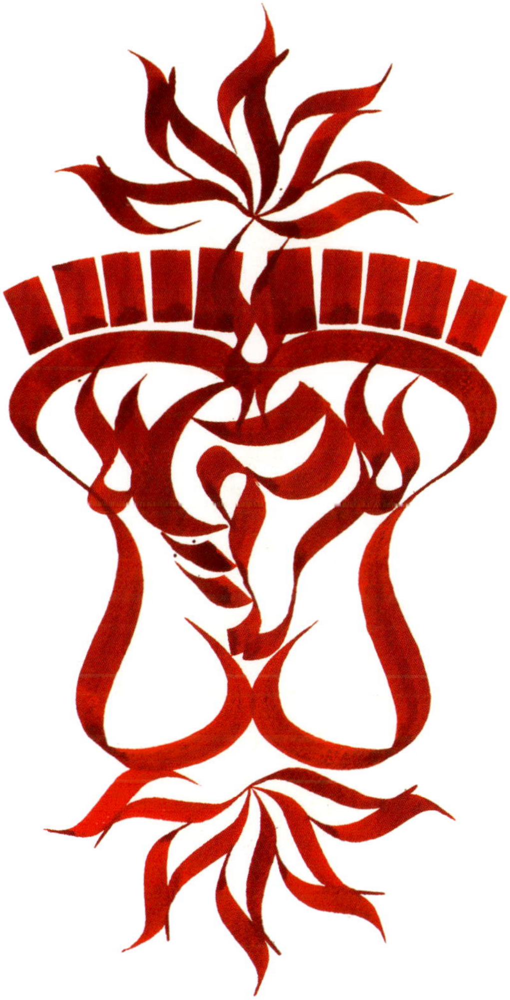

Feet of Vishnu
Calligraphy ink on archival paper, 42 x 30 cm

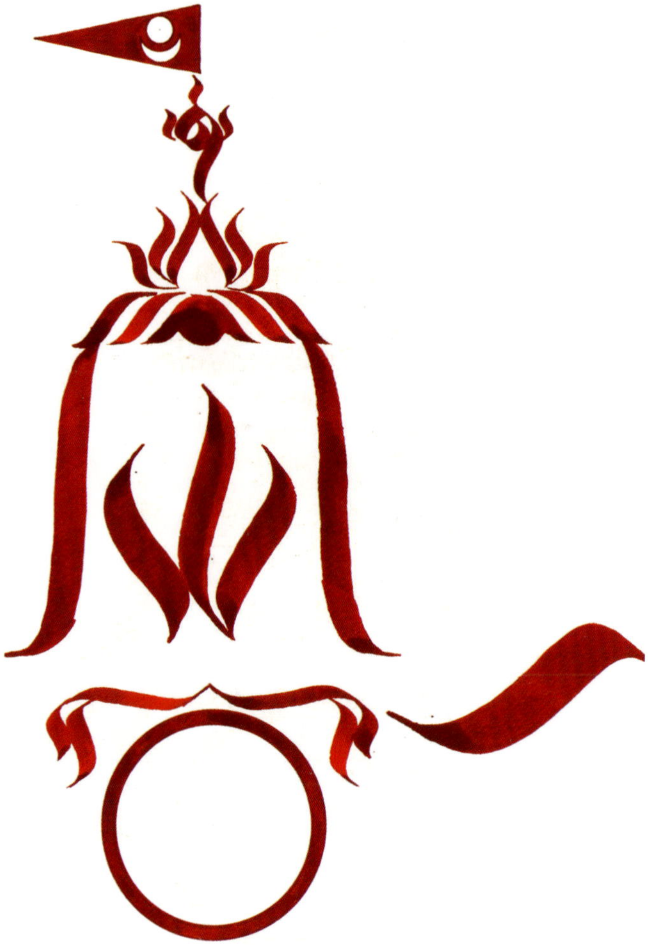

Taladwaja
Calligraphy ink on archival paper, 42 x 30 cm

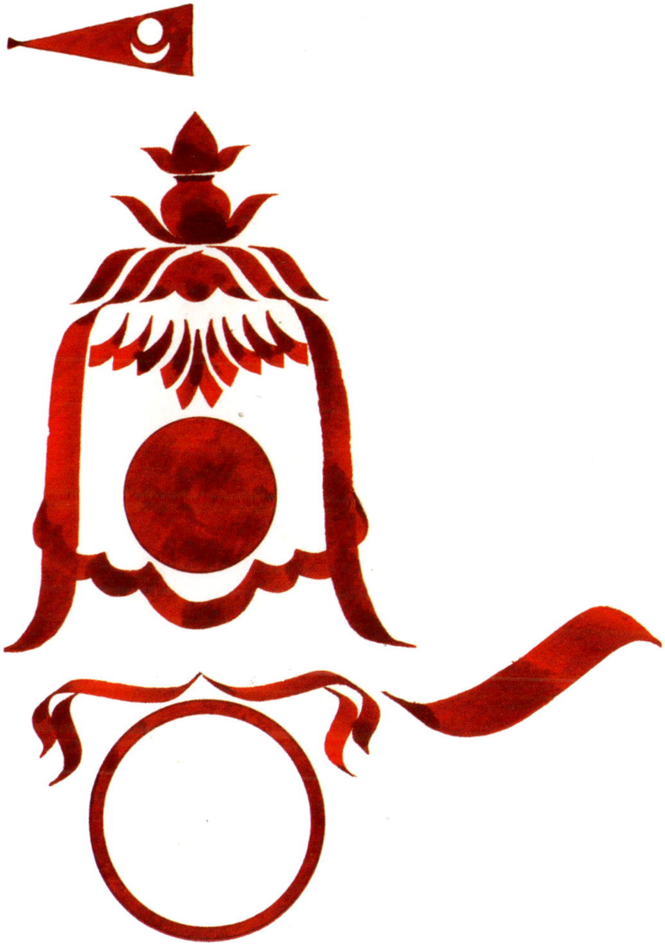

Darpadalana
Calligraphy ink on archival paper, 42 x 30 cm

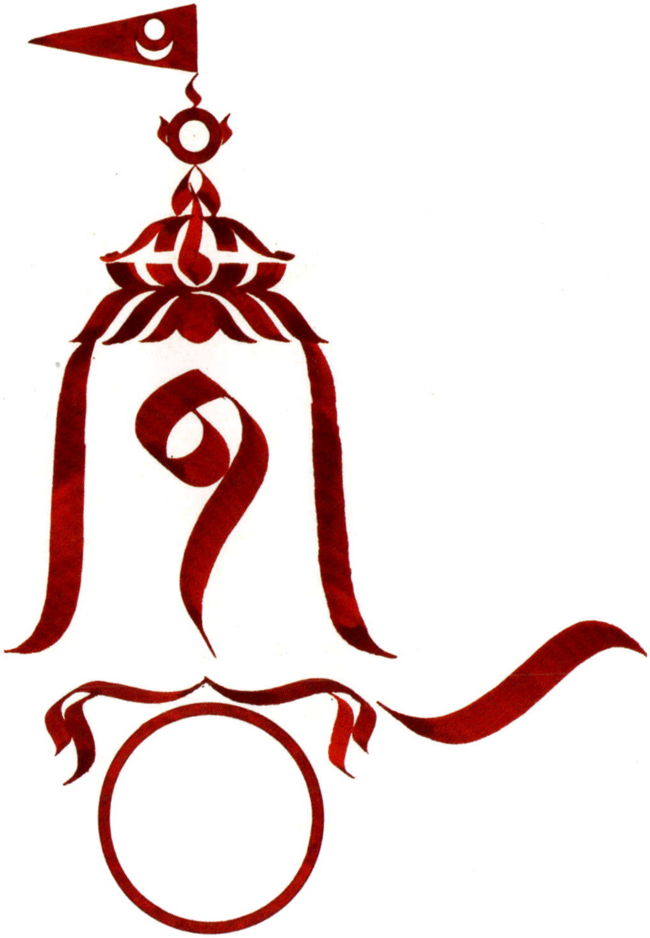

Nandighosa
Calligraphy ink on archival paper, 42 x 30 cm

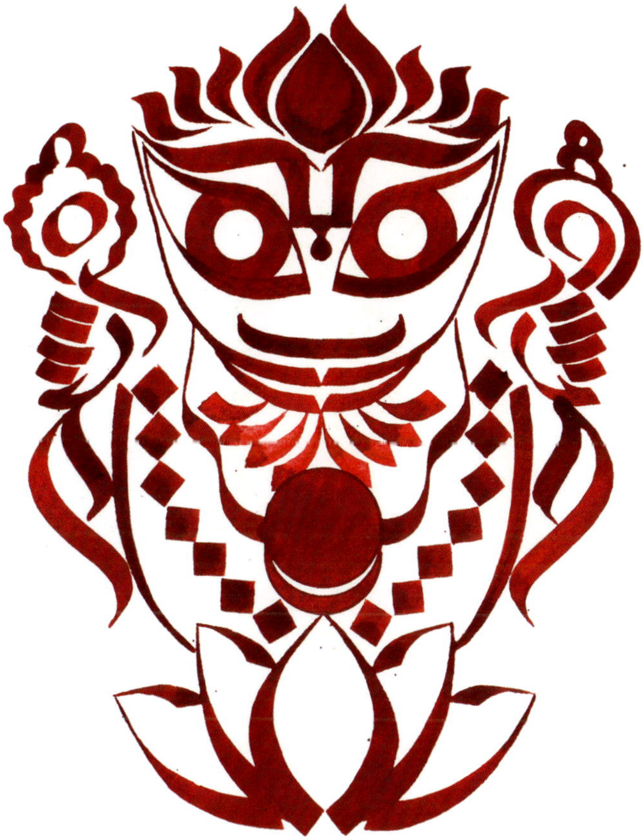

Jagannatha
Calligraphy ink on archival paper, 32 x 24 cm

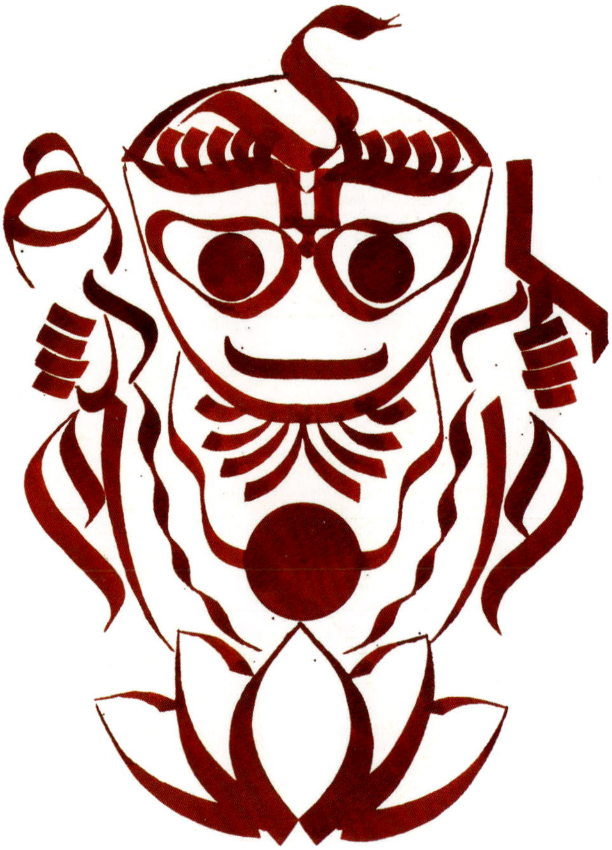

Balabhadra
Calligraphy ink on archival paper, 32 x 24 cm

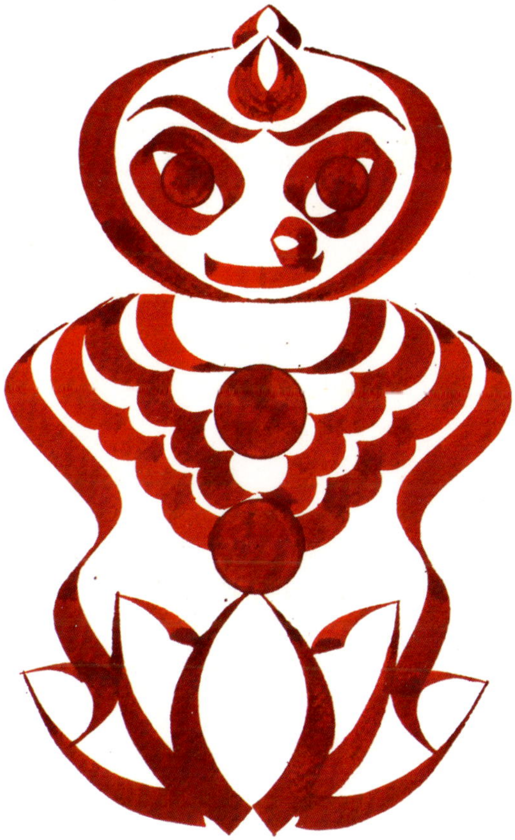

Subhadra
Calligraphy ink on archival paper, 32 x 24 cm

WORLD FAITHS

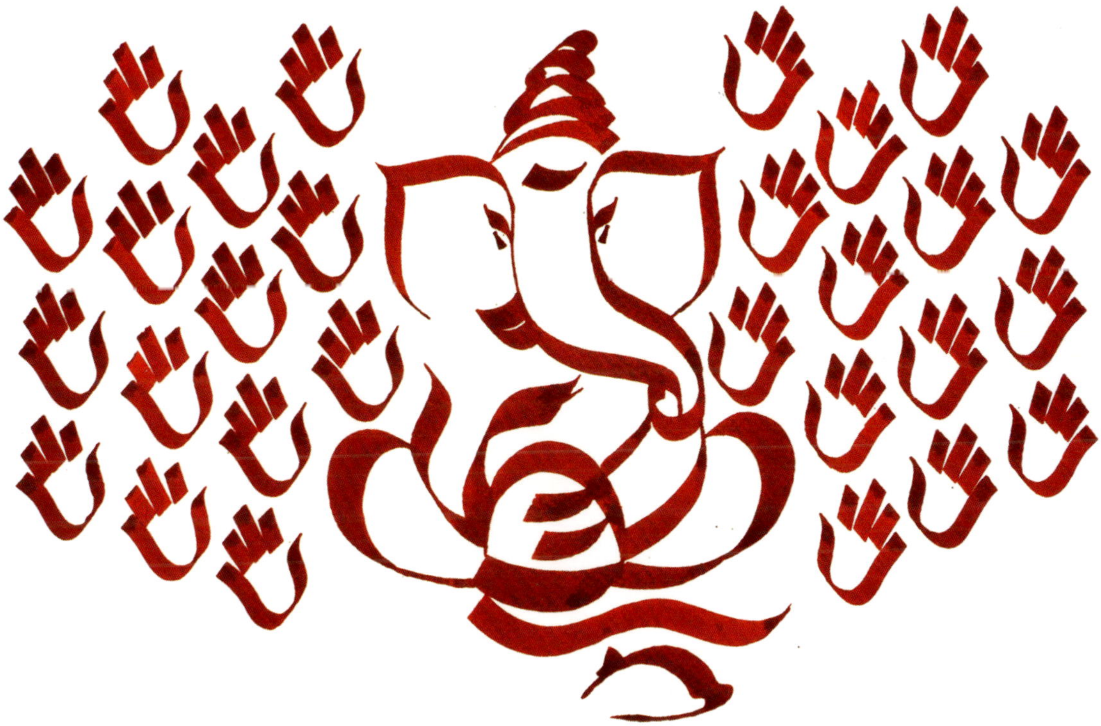

Blessings of Ganesha – Hinduism
Calligraphy ink on archival paper, 30 x 42 cm

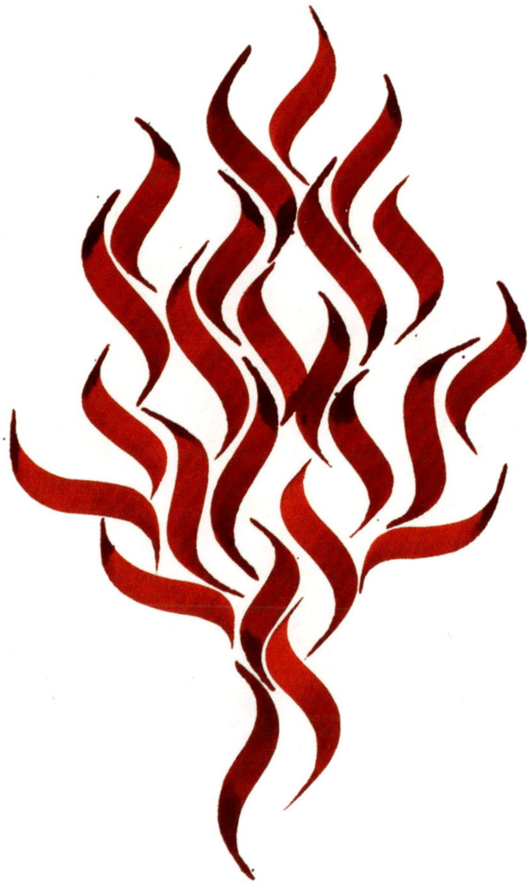

Benign perch of sublimation – Hinduism
Calligraphy ink on archival paper, 32 x 24 cm

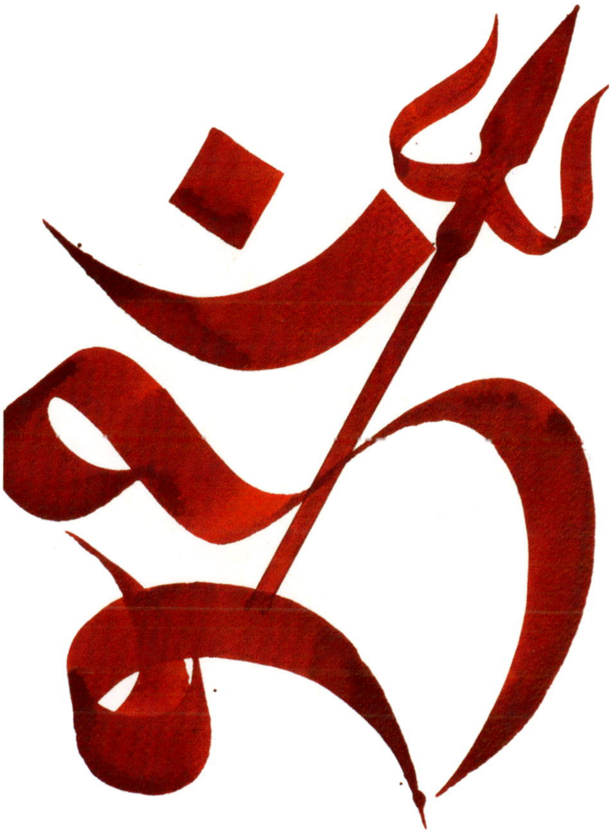

Mahishasuramardini – Hinduism
Calligraphy ink on archival paper, 32 x 24 cm

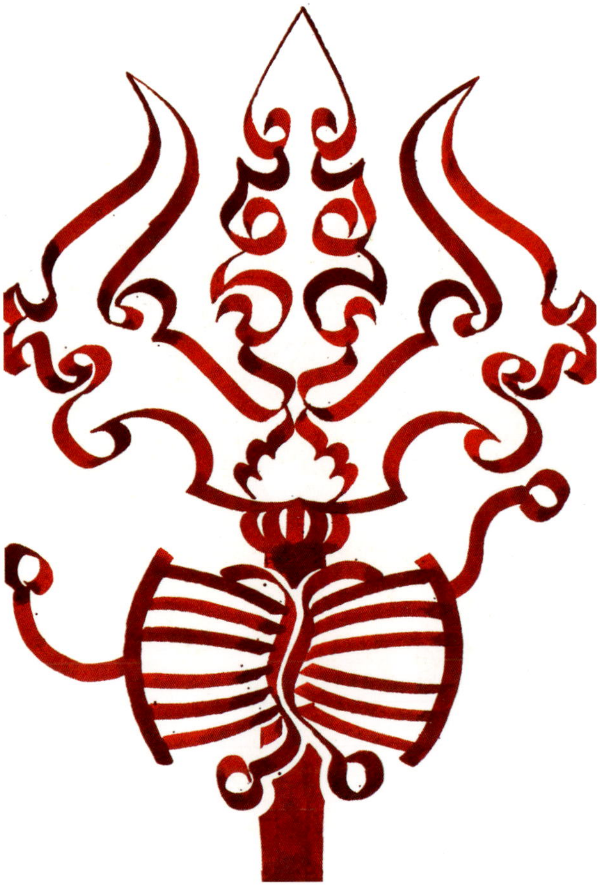

Shiva – Hinduism
Calligraphy ink on archival paper, 32 x 24 cm

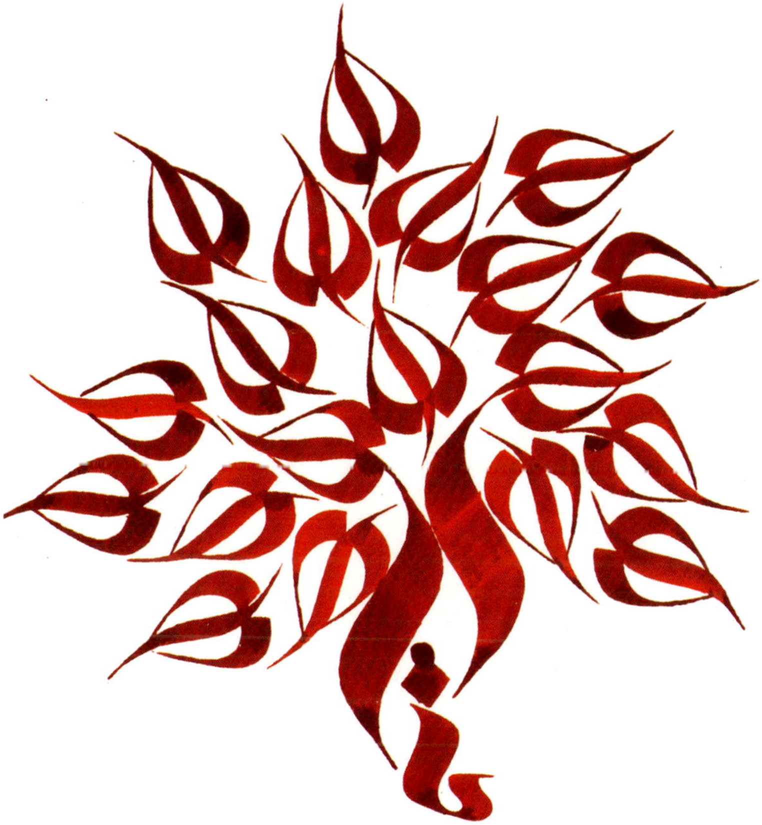

Buddha under the Bodhi tree – Buddhism
Calligraphy ink on archival paper, 42 x 30 cm

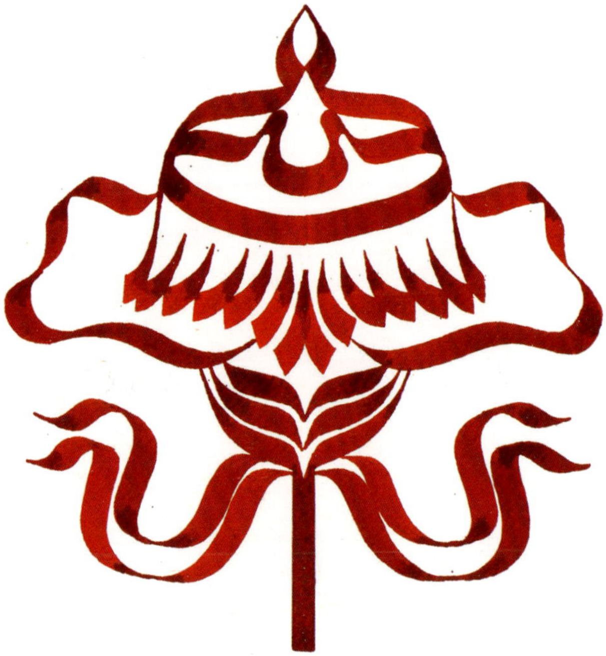

Chatra – Buddhism
Calligraphy ink on archival paper, 32 x 24 cm

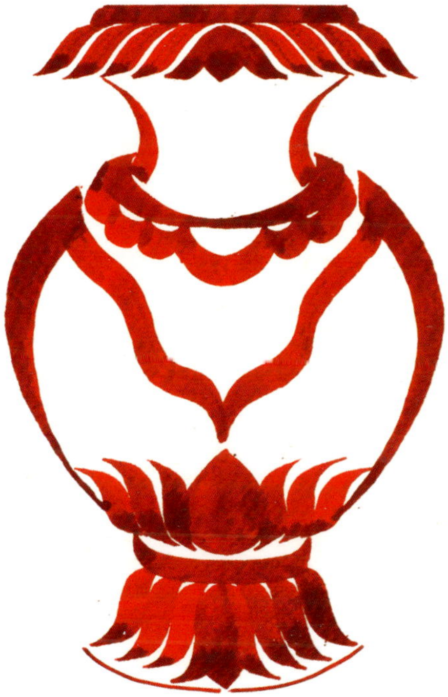

Kalasha – Buddhism
Calligraphy ink on archival paper, 32 x 24 cm

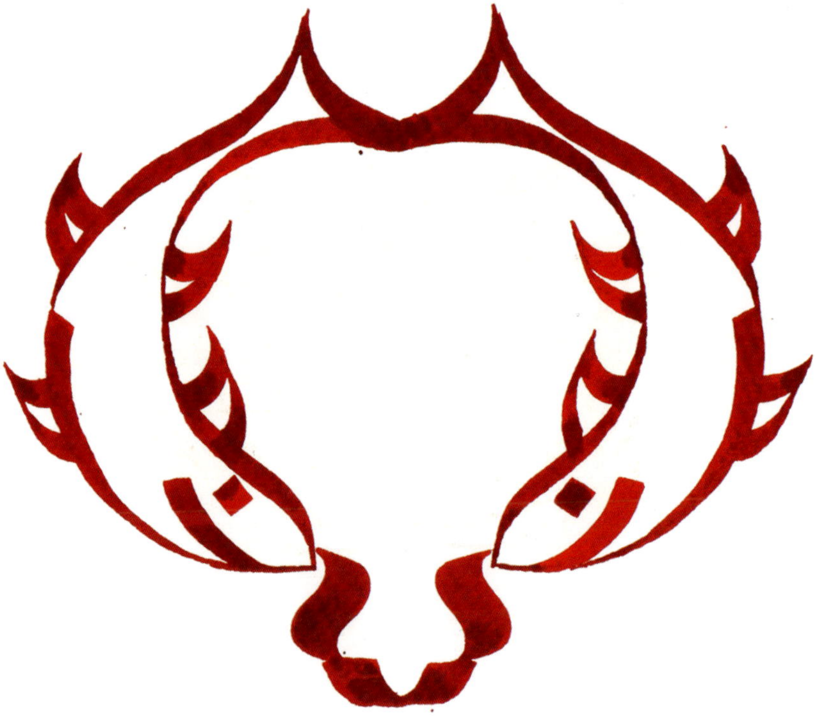

Suvarna Matsya – Buddhism
Calligraphy ink on archival paper, 32 x 24 cm

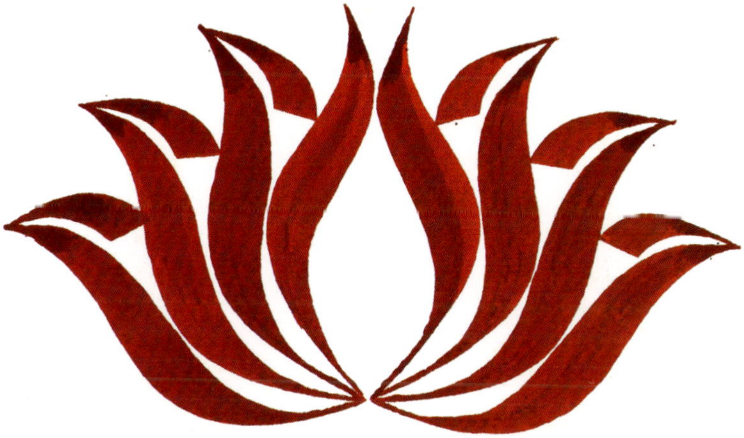

Padma – Buddhism
Calligraphy ink on archival paper, 32 x 24 cm

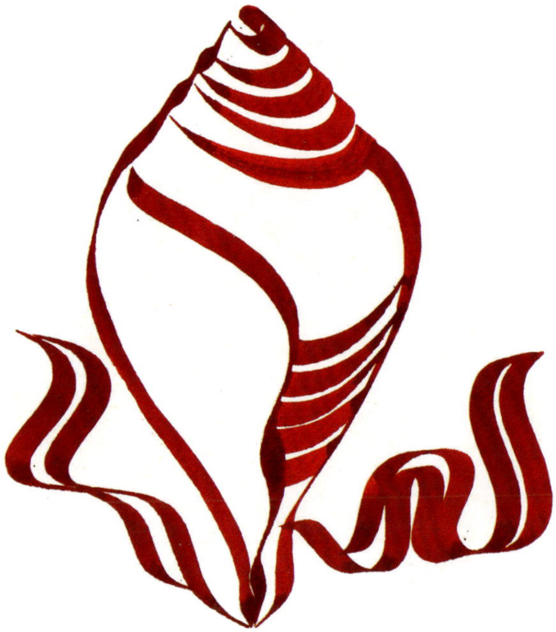

Shankh – Buddhism
Calligraphy ink on archival paper, 32 x 24 cm

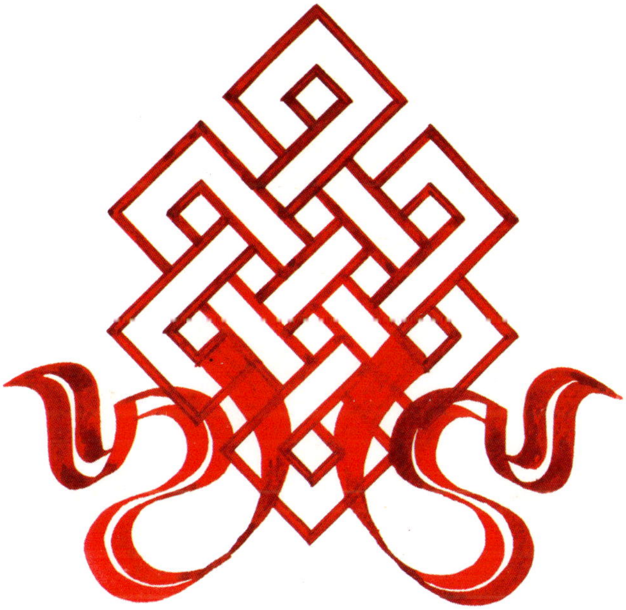

Srivatsa – Buddhism
Calligraphy ink on archival paper, 32 x 24 cm

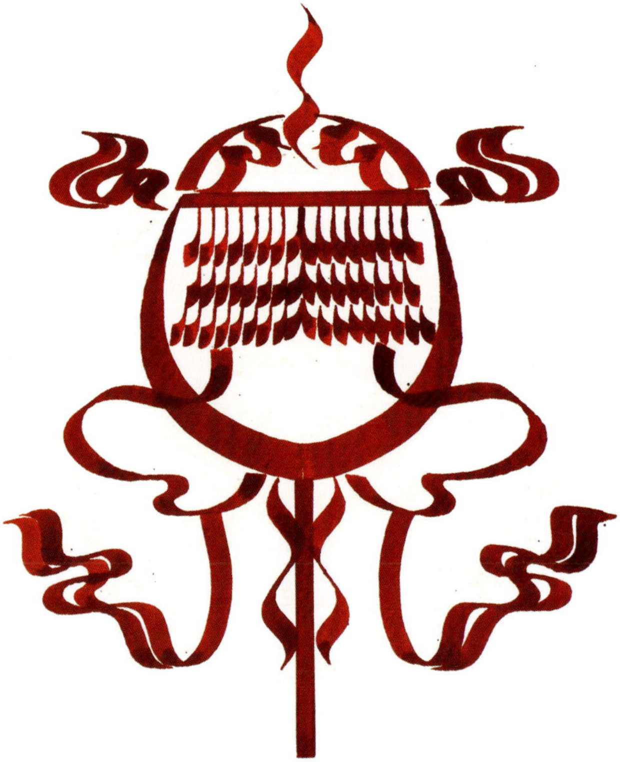

Dhvaja – Buddhism
Calligraphy ink on archival paper, 32 x 24 cm

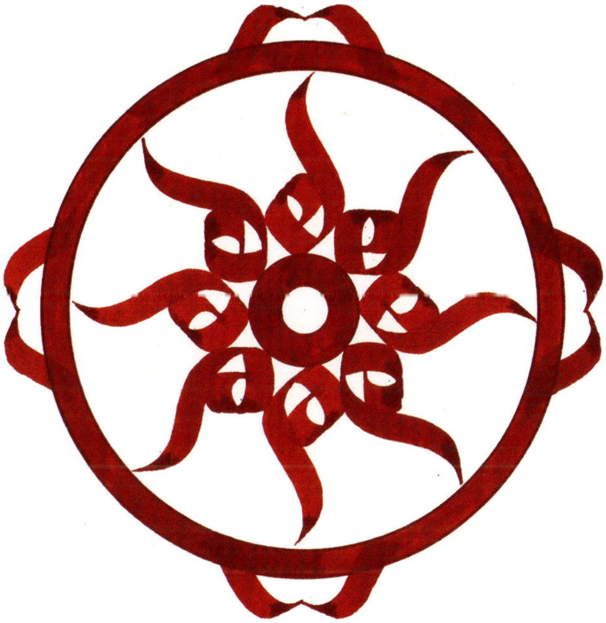

Dharmachakra – Buddhism
Calligraphy ink on archival paper, 32 x 24 cm

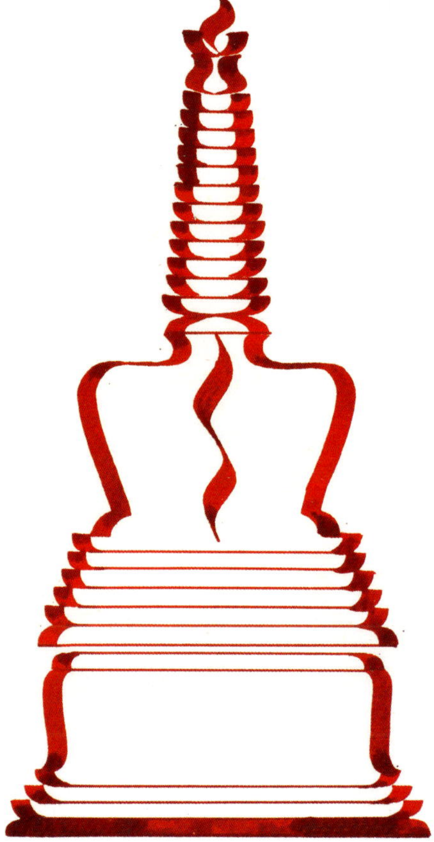

Stupa – Buddhism
Calligraphy ink on archival paper, 32 x 24 cm

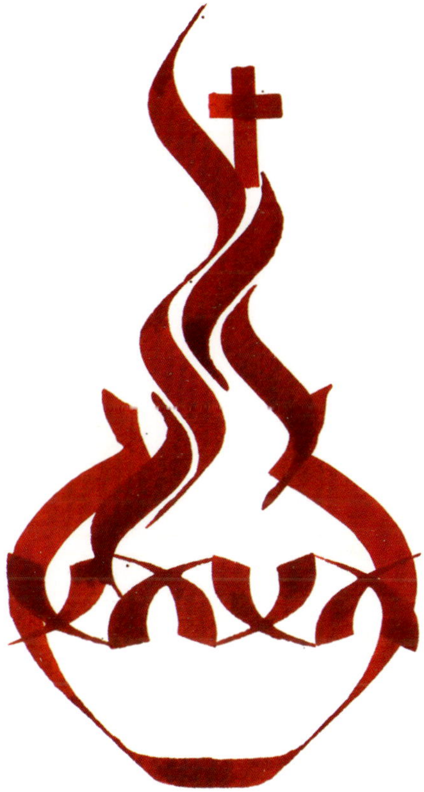

Sacred Heart – Christianity
Calligraphy ink on archival paper, 32 x 24 cm

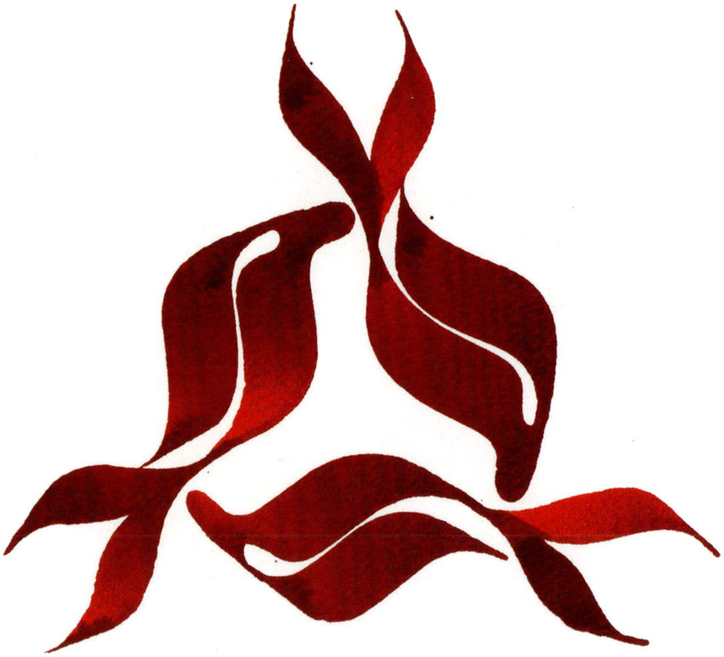

Triquetra – Christianity
Calligraphy ink on archival paper, 32 x 24 cm

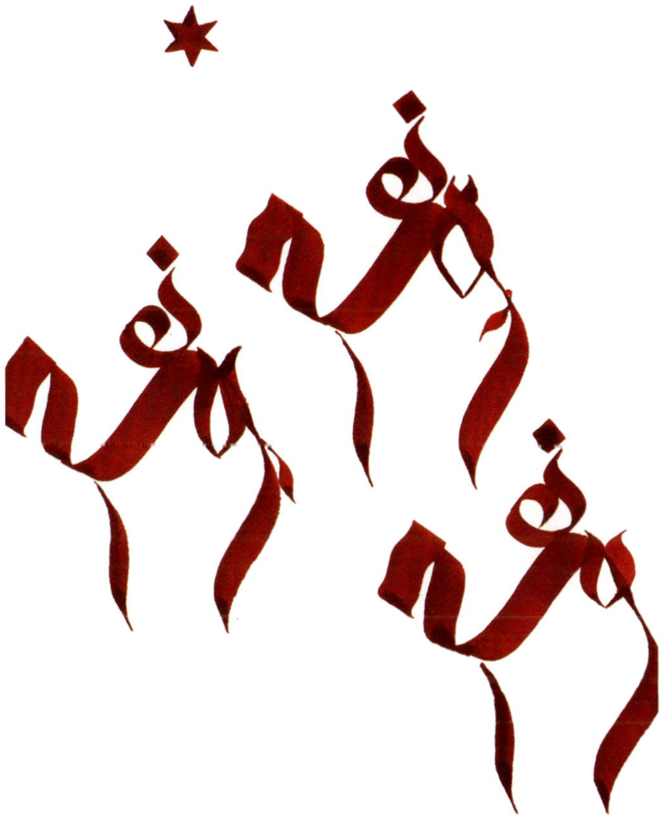

Three Wise Men – Christianity
Calligraphy ink on archival paper, 42 x 30 cm

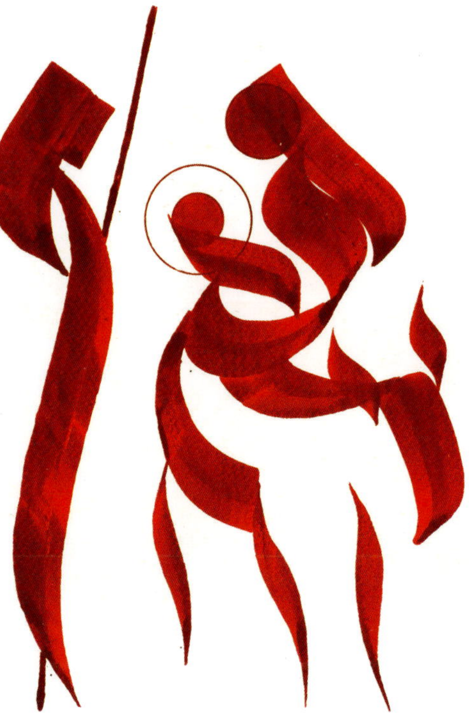

The flight of the holy family to Egypt – Christianity
Calligraphy ink on archival paper, 42 x 30 cm

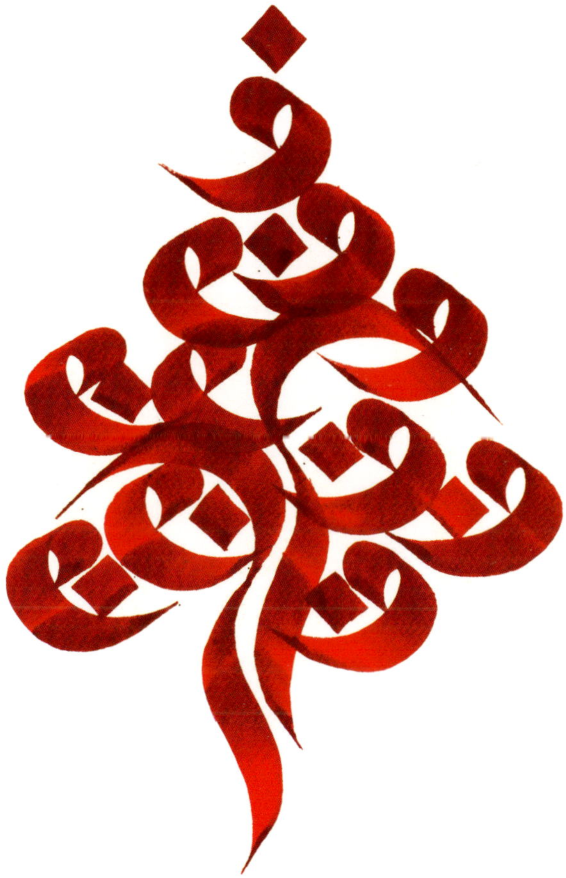

Christmas tree – Christianity
Calligraphy ink on archival paper, 42 x 30 cm

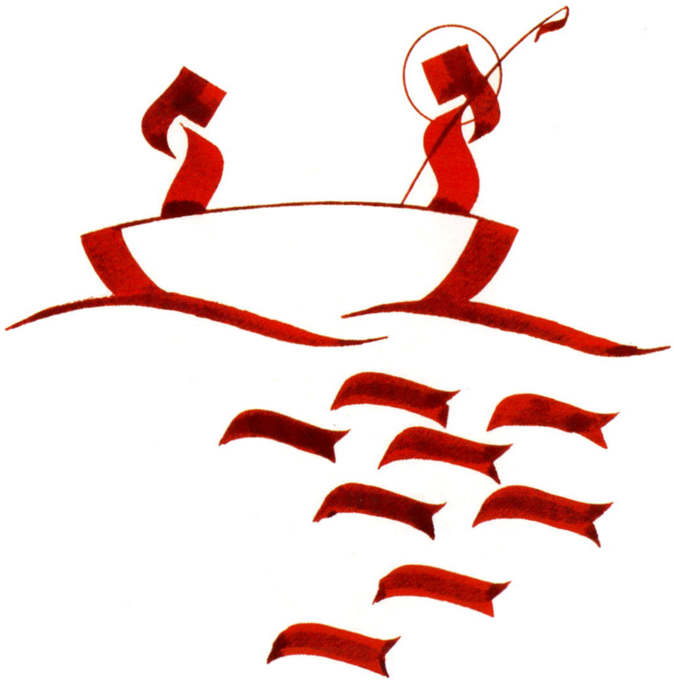

Simon and Jesus – Christianity
Calligraphy ink on archival paper, 42 x 30 cm

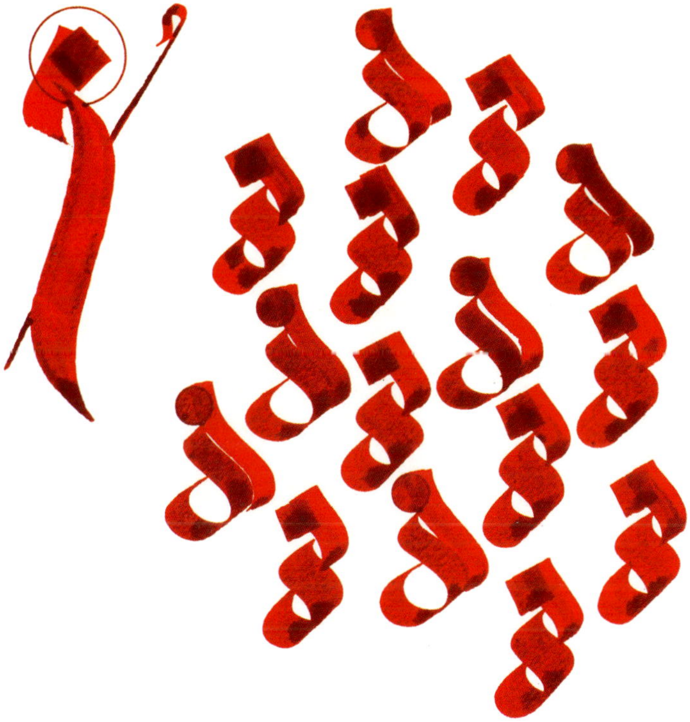

The Sermon on the Mount – Christianity
Calligraphy ink on archival paper, 42 x 30 cm

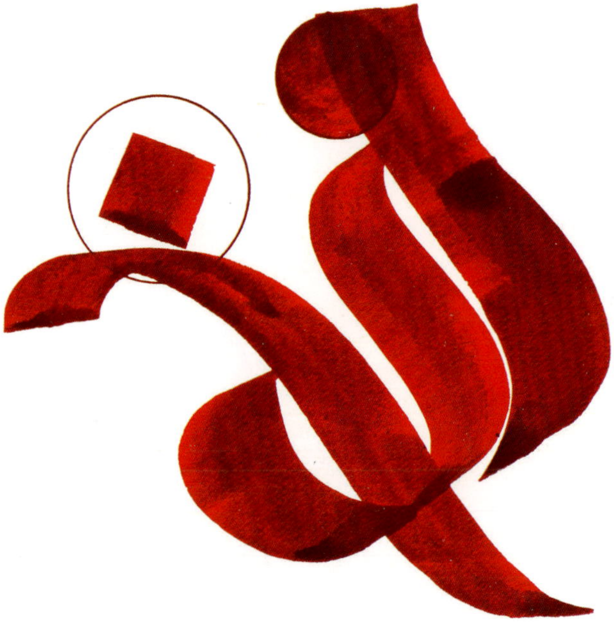

Pieta – Christianity
Calligraphy ink on archival paper, 42 x 30 cm

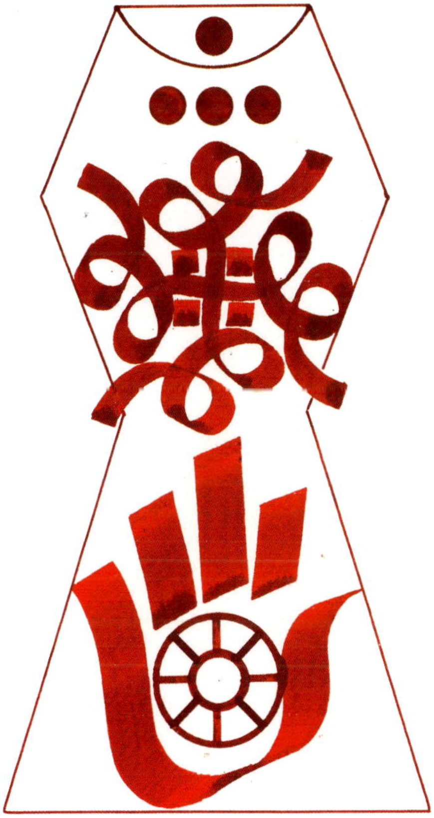

Parasparopagraha Jeevanam – Jain
Calligraphy ink on archival paper, 32 x 24 cm

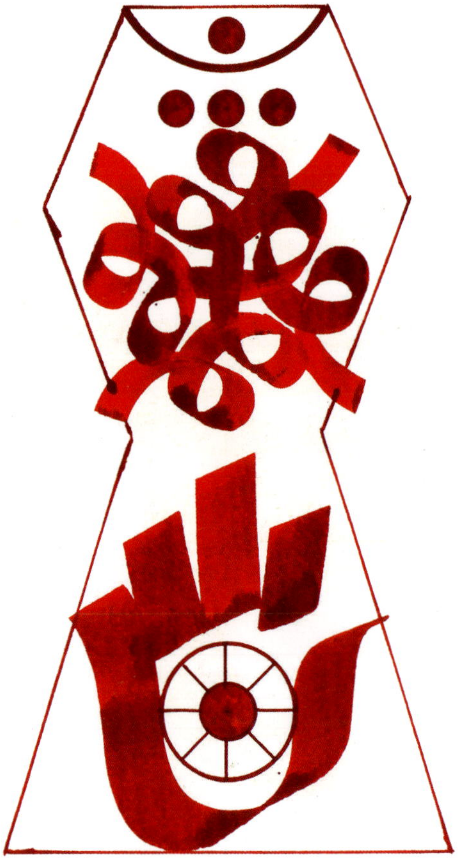

Parasparopagraha Jeevanam – Jain
Calligraphy ink on archival paper, 32 x 24 cm

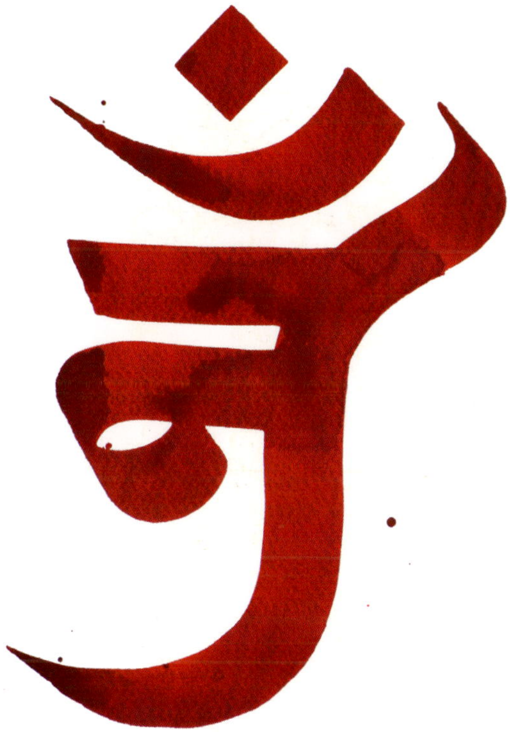

Namo – Jain
Calligraphy ink on archival paper, 30 x 40 cm

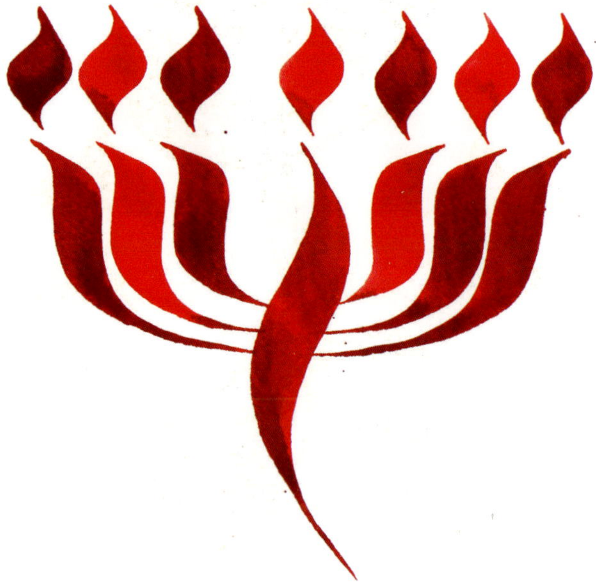

Menorah – Jewish
Calligraphy ink on archival paper, 42 x 24 cm

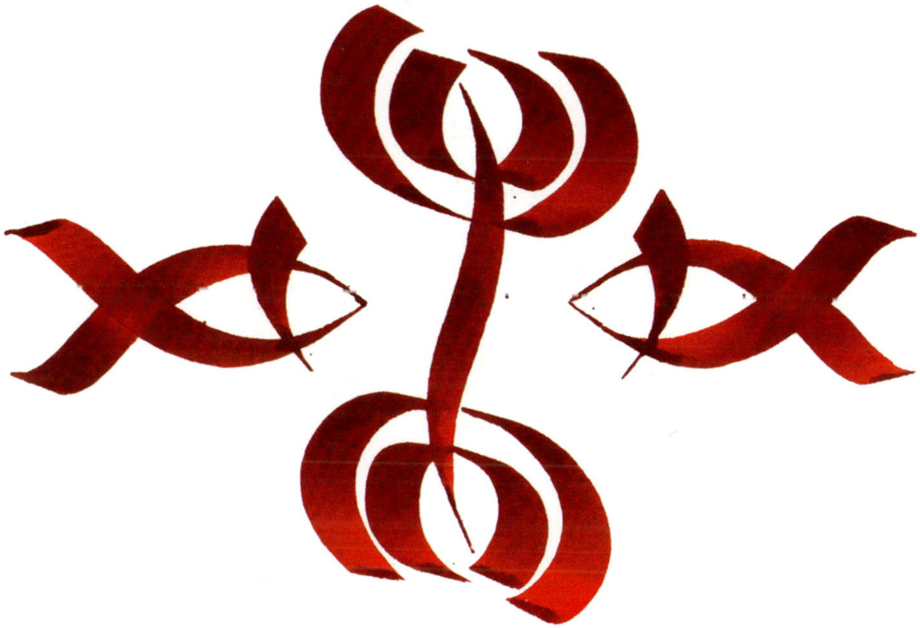

Candle and fish – Jewish
Calligraphy ink on archival paper, 24 x 32 cm

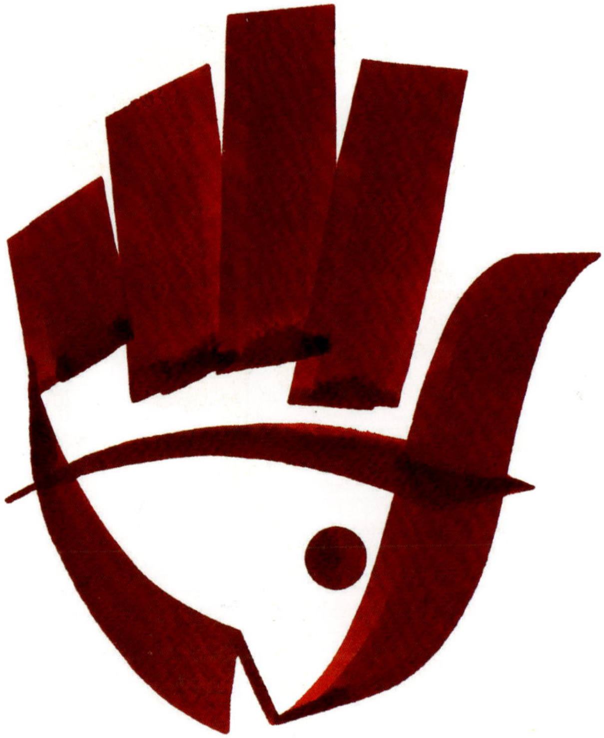

The hand of Fatima – Jewish
Calligraphy ink on archival paper, 32 x 24 cm

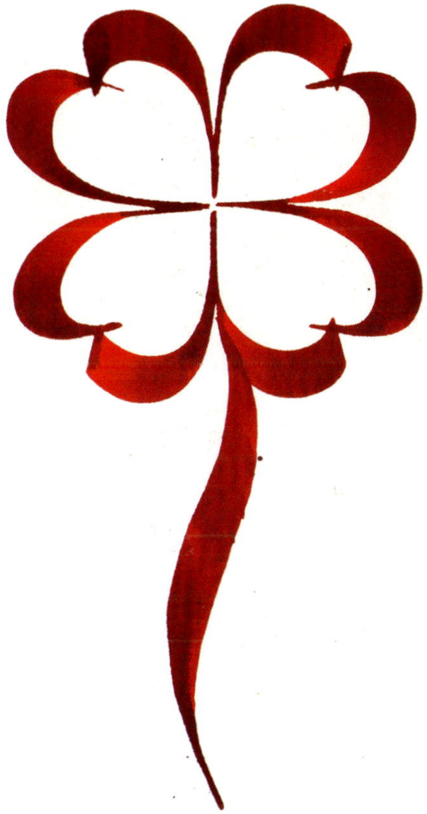

Flower with four petals – Jewish
Calligraphy ink on archival paper, 32 x 24 cm

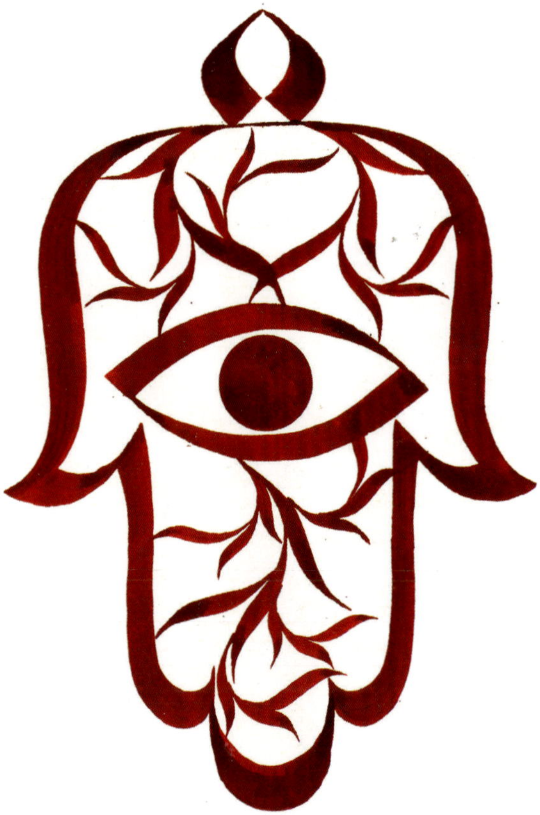

Hamsa – Jewish
Calligraphy ink on archival paper, 32 x 24 cm

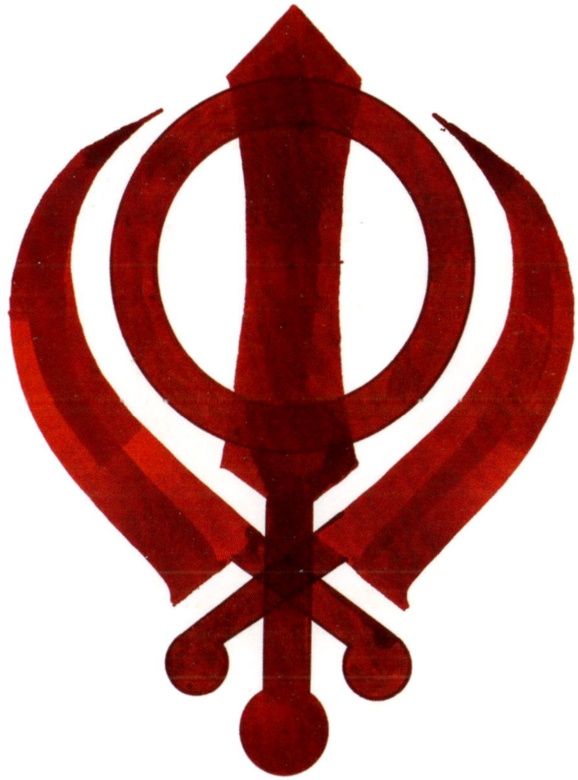

Khanda – Sikhism
Calligraphy ink on archival paper, 32 x 24 cm

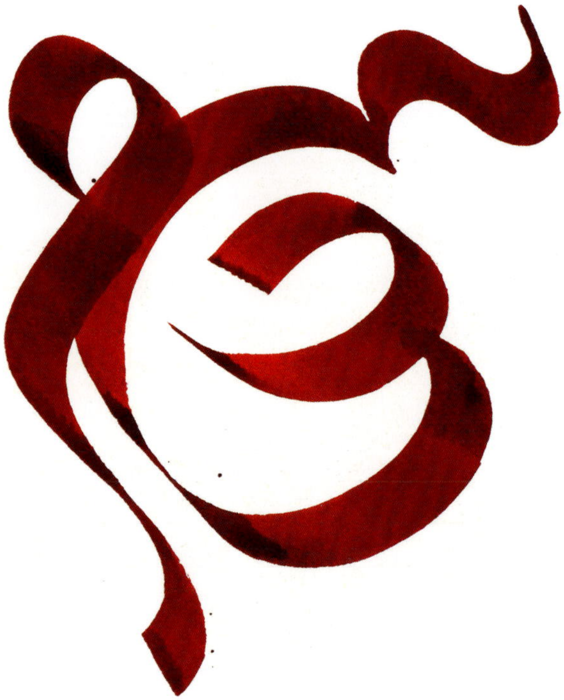

The hand of Fatima – Sikhism
Calligraphy ink on archival paper, 32 x 24 cm

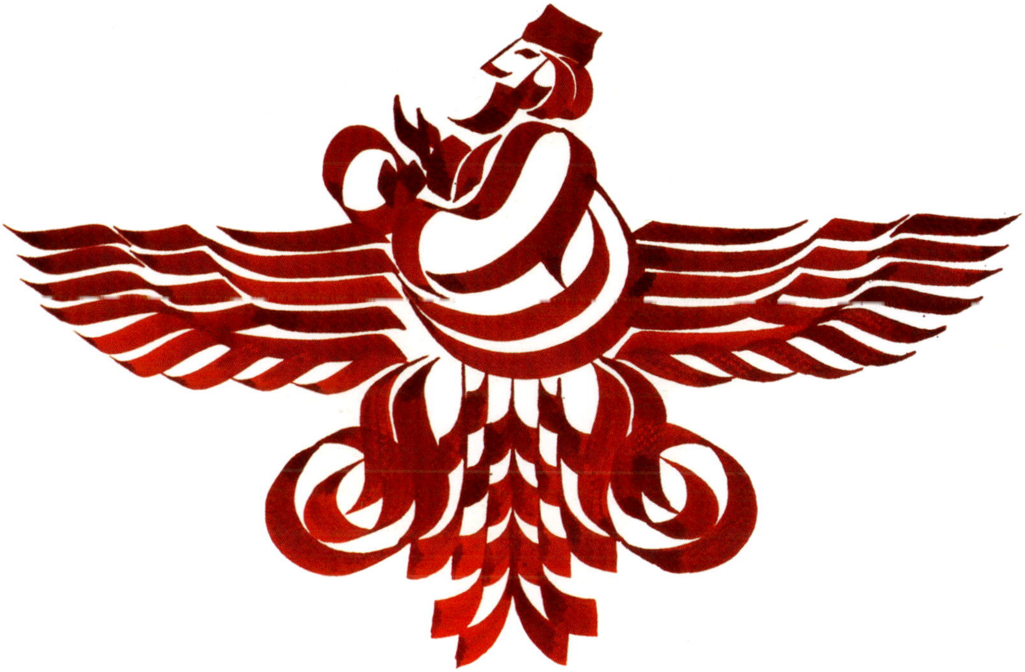

Ahura Mazda – Zoroastrian
Calligraphy ink on archival paper, 30 x 40 cm

NOTES ON SOME OF THE ARTWORK

Ramayana

p24 Queen Kaikeyi listens to her maid Manthara advocating that the queen request her husband, King Dasaratha, to grant her the two boons he had long ago promised her. Manthara advises that the boons should be: 1) exile Rama to the forest for fourteen years, and 2) announce that Kaikeyi's son, Bharata, be anointed as the Crown Prince of Ayodhya.

p33 Jatayu tries to stop Ravana, but Ravana severs one of his wings, thus forcing him to succumb. Sita drops her ornaments all along the route of her abduction, leaving clues for Rama to follow.

p34 In search of Sita, Rama and Lakshmana reach the Rishyamukha mountain. Sugriva, who has seen Rama and Lakshmana, sends Hanuman to find out who they are. After a satisfying exchange with Rama, Hanuman bows before him and forms an alliance between Rama and Sugriva.

p35 Sugriva, Vali's brother, had dethroned Vali and taken away his queen. Rama sympathizes with Sugriva and decides to help him. Vali is indomitable, so when Vali and Sugriva confront each other, Rama shoots his arrow from behind Vali and destroys him. Rama then announces Sugriva as the King of Kishkindha, and Vali's son Angada, as prince regent. Sugriva reciprocates by helping Rama in his search for Sita.

p36 As Hanuman crosses over to Lanka, he encounters a sea-monster, Surasa, who challenges him to enter her mouth. Hanuman has the power to increase and decrease his own form at will. He reduces his own size and goes into Surasa's gaping mouth and then grows monumental within Surasa and emerges, as Surasa cannot contain him. When Hanuman outwits her, she admits that her challenge was merely a test of his courage.

p37 In the Ramayana, Hanuman changes his shape several times. While he searches for the abducted Sita in Ravana's palaces at Lanka, he reduces himself to the size of a cat so that he will not be noticed by the enemy. Later on, to show his true power to Sita, he becomes as big as a mountain, blazing with radiance.

p38 After meeting Sita, Hanuman begins to cause devastation, gradually destroying the palaces and properties of Lanka and killing many rakshasas. To subdue him, Ravana's son Indrajit uses the brahmastra weapon. Although unaffected, Hanuman allows himself to be bound out of respect for Brahma, to make use of the chance to meet Ravana, and to assess the strength of Ravana and his army. Hanuman thus lets the rakshasa warriors parade him through the streets. He then conveys to them Rama's demand for the safe return of Sita, and he also informs Ravana that Rama will be willing to forgive him if he returns Sita honorably.

p39 The infuriated Ravana orders the execution of Hanuman, at which point Ravana's brother (Vibhishana) intervenes, pointing out that it is against the rules of political engagement to kill a messenger. Ravana then orders Hanuman's tail to be set on fire. As Ravana's forces attempt to wrap cloth around Hanuman's tail, Hanuman began to lengthen it. After frustrating them for a while, he allows his tail to be set on fire, but he then escapes, and with his tail on fire burns down large portions of Lanka.

p44 In search of the sanjivani herb to revive Lakshman, Hanuman fetches the Dronagiri mountain from the Himalayas. Since many of the Vanarasena have succumbed to their injuries, a large supply of the herb is needed to prepare enough medicine. Therefore Hanuman brings the entire mountain to serve all who were injured, along with Lakshmana.

p45 Much to the trepidation of Indra, Kumbhakarna (brother of Ravana) is considered pious, intelligent, and brave. Along with his brothers, Ravana and Vibhishana, he performs a major sacrifice to Lord Brahma. When the time comes for asking for a boon from Brahma, on Indra's request, Kumbhakarna's tongue is tied by goddess Saraswati. So instead of asking for Indrasana (the seat of Indra), he asked for nidrasana, a bed for sleeping. Kumbhakarna also intended to ask for nirdevatam (annihilation of the Devas), but he instead asks for nidravatam (sleep). His request is granted. But his brother Ravana asks Brahma to undo this boon, as it is in reality a curse. So Kumbhakarna sleeps for only six months out of every year.

During the war, Ravana goes into battle, but is embarrassed by Rama and his army. He decides he needs the help of his brother, Kumbhakarna, who is awakened, although he could not complete his six months of sleep. When informed of the circumstances of Ravana's war with Rama, Kumbhakarna tries to convince Ravana to comply with Rama's demand, but Ravana pays no heed. Kumbhakarna devastates Rama's army, injures Hanuman and knocks Sugriva unconscious, taking him as a prisoner of war. But because Kumbhakarna is weak from insufficient sleep, he is defeated and killed by Rama.

Krishna

p55 Krishna and his friends reach out for the pot of butter while Radha and Vishakha looks on.

p57 Lord Krishna is the master of the finer aspects of artistry and performance. He plays his flute while the cows graze, with the strains of divine music trailing far beyond Govardhana hill. The peacocks then come dancing and request Krishna to dance with them. Their music and dance together create an enchanting resonance, heaven and earth witnesses the festival of bliss. The king of the peacocks humbly sheds his plumes as guru-dakshina and Sri Krishna wears them in his turban.

p58 The Gopikas complain to Yashoda that Krishna gathered all their saris and sat on the treetop while they were bathing and would not come down even after being called. As in all of Krishna's lila, this event is symbolic. To realize the Lord, the Gopikas had to abandon attachment to the body so as to realize that the body is just a vessel that contains the spirit.

p59 Nanda had 900, 000 cows, 108 herds and the leader of each herd had a name. Lord Krishna would call out for Dhavali (the name of a white cow) and a whole group of white cows would come to him. The Lord would call for Hamsi, Candani, Ganga, Mukta – by their names and twenty-four other groups of white cows would respond. Red cows were called Aruni, Kumkuma, and Saraswati. Shyamala, Dhumala, and Yamuna were black cows and Pita, Pingala, and Haritaki were yellow cows.

p62 The representation of Venkateshvara by the elaboration of the urdhva pundra, or the sign of the Vishnu namam, depicting the eyes of the Lord by placing the shankha and chakra to adapt the role of a signifier as an embodiment of Vishnu. This selective stylization creates forms or insignias that are characteristically minimal, imbibe narration and are integral to its own meaning.

p63 This symbol indicates the presence of Vishnu. Pundarikaksha means the lotus eyed one. The Vishnu namam, or tilak, is the sandal paste mark on the ajna chakra of Vishnu and is constructed by three vertical strokes suggestive of the form of a blooming lotus. The capacious shankha, held by Vishnu, is the sign of fertility, victory of good over evil, and heralding of good tidings.

p64 The presence of Vishnu is symbolized by the pundarikaksha namam, the auspicious sign on the forehead of Vishnu and the chakra. The chakra was gifted to Vishnu by Shiva. It symbolizes the wheel of energy that destroys evil and preserves the universe.

p66 The chariot of Lord Balabhadra is driven by Sarathi Daruka. The flag is distinct with a palm tree symbol. It has fourteen wheels, each seven feet in diameter, and is covered with red and blue cloth. The chariot is forty-four feet high and drawn by a white horse. The Parsva Devata guards the entrance of the chariot.

p67 The chariot of Subhadra is known as Darpadalana, which means trampler of pride. It is forty-three feet high with twelve wheels, each seven feet in diameter. This chariot is decked with a covering of red and black cloth, black being traditionally associated with Shakti and the Mother Goddess. Drawn by red horses, the chariot is driven by Arjuna – Subhadra's husband. Parsva Devata guards the entrance of the chariot.

p68 Lord Jagannatha's chariot is forty-five feet high and forty-five feet square at the wheel level. It has sixteen wheels, each seven feet in diameter, and is decked with a cover made of red and yellow cloth. Lord Jagannatha is identified with Krishna who is also known as Pitambara, the one attired in golden yellow robes – hence the distinguishing yellow stripes on the canopy of this chariot. It is drawn by a dark horse driven by Matali. The Parsva Devata is present as the guardian god of the chariot.

p69 The meaning of Jagannatha is "Lord of the Universe." He is worshipped as one of the three deities on the jeweled platform in the Puri temple of Odisha. The other two deities are his brother Balabhadra and sister Subhadra. Jagannatha is considered a form of Vishnu.

According to legend, in Satya-yuga, Indradyumna (a king in the lunar dynasty) received a pilgrim who described the great God, Nila Madhava – Blue Vishnu – being worshipped at Nilachal (Blue Mountain) in Odisha. On hearing this, the King requested the royal priest and his younger brother, Vidyapati, to search for Nila Madhava. Vidyapati reached the forest in Savardvipa on the banks of the river Mahanadi. The Savara king, Visvavasu, received Vidyapati and promised to show him Nila Madhava. Vidyapati was following austerities out of devotion to see the divinity. The Savara king had him seated under the Kalpavriksha tree. Vidyapati saw Nila Madhava being worshipped by the Gods. But Indradyumna was not able to see Nila Madhava, as the deity had disappeared.

The King received a divine message from Nila Madhava, "I will manifest in four forms: Jagannatha, Balabhadra, Subhadra, and Sudarshana chakra." In the message, the King was directed to wait near Chakra tirtha for a log to float ashore, and to look out for the signs of shankha, chakra, gada, and padma on that log. Four deities were to be created from the log. And this would enable King Indradyumna to worship Jagannatha, Balabhadra and Subhadra. Due to the King's ardent devotion, God came in the form of Visvakarma and made the idols from the wood. Vishvakarma had a condition that the door of the temple should remain shut and nobody must try to enter the temple, or disturb the carpenter, until the deities were ready. However, out of curiosity, the King (or according to alternative versions, Queen Gundicha) could not help stealing a glance at Vishvakarma's work. Vishvakarma, upset at the breach of promise, vanished without completing the deities. Thus, Jagannatha, Balabhadra, and Subhadra are still represented without the realistic detail of the hands and feet. It is believed that Lord Brahma installed the holy deities on an auspicious day in the early days of summer.

p71 Subhadra is the daughter of Vasudeva and Rohini. She is one of three deities worshipped at the Jagannatha temple in Puri, along with her brothers; Krishna (Jagannatha) and Balarama (Balabhadra).

Hinduism

p73 This image is inspired by the story of Ganesha worshipping Shiva, and blessing his devotees with abundant good fortune.

p74 The imagined trees convey a subtle paradigm of the kalpavriksha, with an adapted signification of events and beliefs.

p75 Durga, the mother protector, destroys Mahishasura, the demon of laziness.

p76 Shiva, the fragrant one who makes us grow. Trishula and damaru are the attributes held by Shiva. Trishula represents the three levels of consciousness, and damaru symbolizes the cyclic rhythm of creation and destruction.

Bhuddhism

p77 This image signifies Buddha's emancipation – his enlightenment – visualizing and crystallizing the significant moment as a motif. At Bodh Gaya, the spiritual teacher Siddhartha Gautama, attained enlightenment under an old, and very large, Peepal tree. Bodh Gaya is located about a hundred kilometers from Patna in Bihar. Siddhartha Gautama later became known as Gautama Buddha. In sacred iconography, the Bodhi tree is identifiable by its heart-shaped leaves. Bodhi trees are planted in close proximity to every Buddhist monastery. The Bodhi tree is

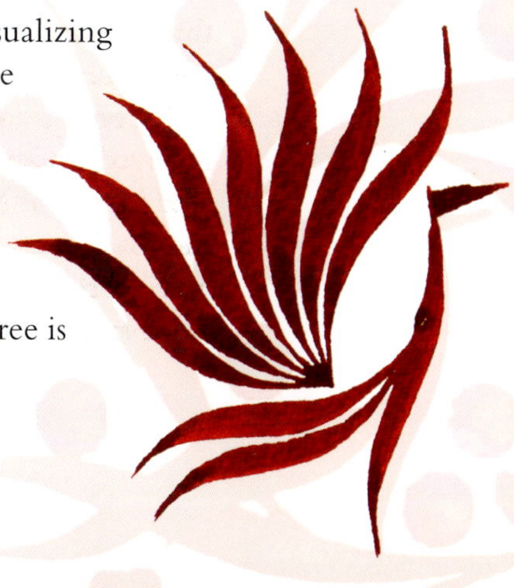

also known as "Bo" in Sri Lanka and "Peepal" in Nepal and Bhutan.

p78 The jeweled parasol, or sacred umbrella, is similar in ritual function to the canopy, a symbolic depiction of sacred medicinal and hallucinogenic mushrooms that are found in the Himalayas; the symbol representing protection from harmful forces or illness. The form symbolizes the sky, or ether, one of the five elements; evocative of the protective quality of the sahasrara. The symbolic layering reinforces the belief that under the auspices of the precious parasol all take refuge in dharma. The chatra is one of the ashtamangala – eight auspicious symbols in Buddhism.

p79 The treasure vase, or urn of wisdom, represents health, longevity, wealth, prosperity, wisdom, and the phenomenon of space with reference to the five mahabhuta (the great elements) and the five pure lights. Space is the essential medium that contains, holds, and conducts all phenomena. The iconographic representation of the "wisdom urn" is similar to that of the "water pot" (Sanskrit: kumbha), which is one of the few allowable possessions of a theravadinbhikku or bhikkuni. The wisdom urn, or treasure vase, is used in Vajrayana initiations and is one of the ashtamangala – eight auspicious symbols in Buddhism.

p80 The sign of two goldfish represents the state of fearless suspension in the ocean of worldliness. Metaphorically it refers to the eyes of Buddha or rigpa-sight; migrating from place to place and teaching freely and spontaneously, akin to the fish that swim without fear in water. The two fish originally represent the two sacred rivers, the Ganga and the Yamuna. These rivers are further associated with the lunar and solar channels, invoking the nadi, the channels of awareness, and prana, the alternating rhythms of breath. In Buddhism, fish symbolize happiness as they have complete freedom of movement. Often drawn in the form of carp, which are regarded in the Orient as sacred because of their elegance, magnitude, and life. The suvarna matsya is one of the ashtamangala – eight auspicious symbols in Buddhism.

p81 The lotus represents the primordial purity of body, speech, and mind. Floating above the muddy waters, the lotus signifies a state of being above attachment and desire. This symbol represents the complete blossoming of honest deeds in delightful emancipation. The padma is one of the ashtamangala – eight auspicious symbols in Buddhism.

p82 The white conch shell represents the deep pervasive melody of Buddhist dharma. This melody awakens the disciple from the slumber of ignorance and urges them to achieve wellbeing and happiness for others and themselves. The shankha is one of the ashtamangala – eight auspicious symbols in Buddhism.

p83 The propitious mark of srivatsa, represented by a curled bridle, is emblematic of love. The sign further represents the entwining of wisdom and compassion, religious doctrine and secular affairs, wisdom and method, emptiness and need, all arising simultaneously. Srivatsa represents the union of wisdom and compassion in enlightenment. It is also symbolic of the knot that links the ancestors to God in the magical ritual of binding. This knot, or web, metaphorically conveys the principle of interpenetration described in

Buddhist teachings. The srivatsa is one of the ashtamangala – eight auspicious symbols in Buddhism.

p84 The dhvaja, the banner or flag, is a military symbol relevant to ancient Indian warfare. In the Tibetan tradition eleven forms of the victory banner are represented by eleven specific methods for overcoming defilements. Variations of the dhvaja's design can be seen on rooftops of Tibetan monasteries. These symbols represent the Buddha's victory over four maraas. The dhvaja is one of the ashtamangala – eight auspicious symbols in Buddhism.

p85 The wheel of law is connected to the Sakyamuni Buddha and his teachings of dharma as an eightfold path. The wheel represents the mandala and chakra. The dharmachakra is one of the ashtamangala – eight auspicious symbols in Buddhism.

p86 A stupa is a symbol of enlightenment and is one of the earliest icons of Buddhist art and architecture. Stupas are holy monuments that are also used for meditation, designed with profound symbolism and sacred geometry. Since Buddhist relics and other holy objects are placed in the stupas, they emanate blessings and peace. It's sacred and symbolic Buddhist architecture.

Christianity

p87 Representing Christianity, the flaming heart glowing with divine light, wounded by the lance, encircled by the crown of thorns and the holy cross all elude to the manner of Jesus' death. The suggestion of bleeding is poignant. The fire represents the transformative power of divine love. Christian symbolism.

p88 The Triquetra is a three-part interlocking fish symbol that representing the Christian trinity. The word "trinity" comes from the Latin noun trinitas meaning "three are one." The trinity represents the belief that God is one being made up of three distinct persons, who exist in co-equal, co-eternal communion as the Father, Son, and Holy Spirit.

p89 The Magi Greek, magoi, also referred to as the three kings. The Gospel of Mathew mentions that this group of illustrious foreigners came from the east. They visited Jesus after his birth bearing gifts of gold, frankincense, and myrrh. The three gifts led to the widespread assumption that there were three men.

p90 The rage of Herod against the Magi of the east, who had escaped from his power, worsened because of his fears of the divine and majestic infant. This led to the massacre of newborn babies, which led to the flight of the Holy Family from the butchery. They were miraculously saved by an angel who spoke to Joseph in a dream saying, "Arise. Take the young child and his mother and flee to Egypt."

p91 The triangular form of the tree with a support at the base recalls the Christmas tree; the quadrangle at the top represents the star. The tree here is an interlacing font of traversing earth and air, extending itself between man, birds, and creatures.

p92 Jesus was preaching near the Lake of Genesareth (the Sea of Galilee). There he saw two boats at the water's edge. Boarding the one belonging to Simon (later Peter), they moved away from shore. Jesus sat and taught the people from the boat. Later, at the insistence of Jesus, they put out the nets into deep waters and caught a large number of fish. Realizing this to be a miracle they became followers of Jesus.

p93 The Sermon is the longest section of teaching from Jesus in the New Testament, and has been one of the most widely quoted elements of the Gospels. It comprises some of the best identified teachings of Jesus, such as the Beatitudes, and the widely recited Lord's Prayer. To most Christians, the Sermon on the Mount contains the vital belief of Christian discipleship.

The last verse of chapter 5 is considered to be a central point that encapsulates the teaching of the sermon: "Be perfect, as your heavenly Father is perfect," directing his disciples to search for the path towards perfection and the Kingdom of God.

p94 As soon as the sacred body of Jesus was taken down from the cross, the men wrapped him in linen from the knees to the waist, and laid him on a sheet in his mother's arms which, in sorrow and yearning, were stretched out to receive him.

Jainism

p95-96

This symbol, also known as Pratik Chinh, shows that the path to enlightenment follows the basic principles of ahimsa (non-violence), triratna (the three precious jewels of right belief, right knowledge, and right conduct), and parasparopagraha jivanam (helping others). The emblem is composed of many fundamental concepts and symbols. The outline of the image represents the universe, consisting of three realms, as described in Jain scriptures. The upper portion indicates heaven, the middle portion indicates the material world, and the lower portion indicates hell. The semi-circular topmost portion symbolizes siddhashila, a zone beyond the three realms. All of the siddhas, the liberated bodiless souls, forever reside here, liberated from the cycle of life and death.

The three dots at the top under the semi-circle symbolize the triratna. Through these, every creature in this world can become free from the cycle of life and death. The four arms of the swastika symbolize the four destinies; demon, animal, human, and angel. The swastika represents the perpetual nature of the universe, where a creature is destined to one of these four states based on their deeds. The four arms represent four columns of the Jain Sangh: sadhus, sadhvis, shravaks and shravikas, and four characteristics of the soul – infinite knowledge, infinite perception, infinite happiness, and infinite energy.

The symbol of the hand in the lower portion shows fearlessness and symbolizes the feeling of non-violence. The circle in the middle of the hand symbolizes the cycle of reincarnation. The twenty-four spokes represent the preachings from the twenty-four Tirthankars, which can be used to liberate a soul from the cycle of reincarnation. The mantra at the bottom "parasparopagraha jivanam" – "live and let live" means all creatures should help one another.

p97 The Om symbol is used in ancient Jain scriptures to represent the five lines of the navakar mantra, which is the most important part of the daily prayer in the Jain religion. The navakar mantra honors the five panch parmeshtis; the great virtuous entities.

Judaism

p98 The candles on the stand represent flames of God, and seven days – the spiritual essence of Israel.

p99 The candles signify prayer and the fish signify faith.

p100 Talisman for Jewish and Islamic faith; the symbol of the fish suggests the benign presence.

p101 Symbol of life called the "flower of the sun" which is placed directly over Mary's womb. It's appearance heralded the birth of someone great who would inaugurate a new era.

p102 Fatima was the daughter of the prophet, Muhammad. The hand of Fatima symbolizes patience, loyalty, faith, and resistance against difficulties.

Sikhism

p103 The khanda depicts, in an emblematic form, the Sikh doctrine "Deg Tegh Fateh" – "Victory to Charity and Sword." It's an integral design of the Sikh national flag, the Nishan Sahib. A double edged sword called khanda is placed at the top of a Nishan Sahib flag as an ornament. The khanda emblem is an amalgam of three symbols, represented by three different items. A khanda is in the center. The deg, two single-edged swords, or kirpans, is crossed at the bottom and flanks both the khanda and the chakra (a circular disk). The image represents the notion of integration of spiritual and temporal sovereignty.

p104 This is the symbol that represents the One Supreme Reality and is a central belief of Sikh religious philosophy. It is a symbol of the unity of God in Sikhism, and is found on all Sikh scriptures and Gurdwaras. Derived from Punjabi, Ik Onkar is the first phrase in the main chant, referring to the existence of "one constant" – "one God." It is found in the Gurumukhi script and is consequently also part of the Sikh morning prayer, "Japji Sahib." It is a combination of two characters, the numeral "Ik" – one, and the first letter of the word "Onkar" – the constant signifying God. It is also the first letter of the Gurumukhi script.

Zoroastrian

p105 Earlier known as a deity in the Iranian religion; the Zoroaster proclaimed Ahura Mazda as the uncreated God who was wise, benevolent, and good, and who was the creator and upholder of truth. Ahura Mazda is considered to be a supporter and guardian of justice, and the friend of honorable men.